ADMEN
MAD MEN
AND THE REAL WORLD
OF ADVERTISING

Also by Dave Marinaccio:

*All I Really Need to Know I Learned from
Watching Star Trek*

ADMEN
MAD MEN
AND THE REAL WORLD
OF ADVERTISING

Essential Lessons
for Business and Life

DAVE MARINACCIO

Arcade Publishing • New York

First Edition

Arcade Publishing books may be purchased in bulk at special discounts for sales promotion, corporate gifts, fund-raising, or educational purposes. Special editions can also be created to specifications. For details, contact the Special Sales Department, Arcade Publishing, 307 West 36th Street, 11th Floor, New York, NY 10018 or arcade@skyhorsepublishing.com.

Arcade Publishing® is a registered trademark of Skyhorse Publishing, Inc.®, a Delaware corporation.

Visit our website at www.arcadepub.com.
Visit Dave Marinaccio's author page on Facebook.

10 9 8 7 6 5 4 3 2 1

Library of Congress Cataloging-in-Publication Data

Marinaccio, Dave.
  Admen, mad men and the real world of advertising : essential lessons for business and life / Dave Marinaccio. — First edition.
     pages cm
  Includes index.
  ISBN 978-1-62872-572-8 (hardcover : alk. paper); ISBN 978-1-62872-621-3 (ebook)
  1. Marinaccio, Dave. 2. Advertising executives—Biography. 3. Advertising. 4. Marketing. I. Title.
  HF5810.M375A3 2015
  659.1092—dc23
  [B]   2015023965

Cover design execution by Janette Kim
Cover illustration: Shutterstock

Printed in the United States of America

For Al, father, dreamer, Navy man

Special Thanks

Jim Herwitz, Danny Vermillion, Paul Mahon, Carol Mann, Doug Laughlin, Chris Laughlin, Scott Laughlin, Ron Owens.

Contents

Introduction

WOMEN DO NOT BUY *Redbook* because it's filled with douche ads. No one turns on their computer to scan banners. Folks do not watch television to see the Orkin man.

Advertising is an intrusion. An unwanted interloper. A necessary evil. It's the price we pay for television production and to hold down the cost of FiOS. It is the intersection of free speech and free enterprise.

Guess how many advertising impressions the average American receives every day. Go ahead, I'll wait.

The answer is over three thousand. Way over. Every single one of us is bombarded by over three thousand TV spots, radio commercials, billboards, print ads, product packages, bottle labels, car logos, store signs, internet banners, phone apps, pop-ups, social media channels, et cetera. That's three thousand advertising impressions each and every day. It gives new meaning to the phrase "ad infinitum."

Nothing could make me happier. I make my living writing ads. For the past thirty years I have created ads for Pizza Hut, McDonald's, Kraft, Oscar Mayer, Ford, Gillette, IKEA, the National Guard, NAPA, the American Dairy Association, the Weather Channel, Sunkist, MCI, Verizon, Schlitz, Michelob and over a hundred more.

I've worked for agencies big and small, from international giants like J. Walter Thompson to little family-owned shops, to my own place, LMO Advertising. The "M" in LMO stands for Me.

I didn't start out as an adman. After graduating from the University of Connecticut, I took a job with the state Department of Mental Health. We weren't in advertising, but we had a slogan. According to a coworker, we were "Committed people committed to committed people."

The Department of Mental Health is actually a great place to apprentice for a career in advertising. Working with mentally disabled adults forces you to keep things simple. Communication must be focused and clear. Being positive and upbeat enhances responses to your message. These lessons have served me well.

Of course, once employed by an ad agency, I learned other lessons. The most basic one was this: advertising is not created to sell products to consumers. It is created to sell advertising to clients of advertising agencies. That is how we make our money.

Common sense dictates that we work this way. No consumer will ever see an ad if a client doesn't purchase it. So advertising that appeals to the client first—and the consumer second—is at the top of an agency's agenda.

Sometimes the consumer never enters into it. A brand manager may need to solve a political problem. Or the ad might be targeted at a competitor. On occasion, the brand manager just wants to work with a certain television director or impress his girlfriend. Alas, this is more common than the advertisers or agencies like to believe.

When I worked on King Edward Cigars, our media director found television programming that perfectly matched the King Edward demographic. There was one small problem. The president of King Edward Cigars refused to advertise on the show.

The show was professional wrestling. El Presidente didn't want anything to do with wrestling. He considered it lowbrow. Never mind that most of the cigars we were selling had a price point of around a nickel.

He suggested we purchase time on the World Series. The series is an extremely expensive media buy. He could have bought a much larger wrestling package for the few spots we aired on the series. Didn't matter.

How did he come to this decision? My guess is that he didn't want to tell his friends that he was sponsoring wrestling. The World Series is a prestigious event. Our respected and beloved client was more concerned with his self-image than he was about selling cigars.

So did the agency buy time on the World Series and take the media commission? Did Monet paint water lilies? You can also bet that everybody on the account told their friends to look for our King Edward spots on the World Series.

Of course, when the World Series ended the baseball fans ran into the streets, turned over cars and set them ablaze. Perhaps they used those flaming cars to light their King Edward cigars. Irony can be pretty ironic. I can't imagine wrestling fans ever acting this lowbrow.

Anyway, when you hear that advertising is a science, take it with a truckload of salt. People are involved, and people make strange choices.

Although this is manifestly an advertising book, it is written from many different perspectives. Anyone who works in a business environment should find it useful. There are sections on being a good client, a good boss, a good underling and a good vender. It also functions as a survival guide for navigating the corporate maze. Other parts are just interesting stories or observations.

As you get into the guts of this book, you'll realize that working in advertising for so many years has made it difficult for me to write long-format pieces. Thirty-second television commercials are more my milieu. Hence, the chapters in this book are extremely short. They are bite size, like McNuggets, and hopefully as tasty.

Like most copywriters, my mind is chaotic and prone to tangents. I have succumbed to those tendencies in this book. The chapters don't follow a prescribed order. They were written as they came to me. Each is like a stroke in an

Impressionistic painting: when you view them together, you will understand the whole.

So, welcome to my world. I can describe advertising only as I've seen and experienced it. I promise to be honest with you—at least as honest as you can expect an adman to be. And I sincerely hope you will find this book nearly as amusing as I've found my career.

ADMEN
MAD MEN
AND THE REAL WORLD
OF ADVERTISING

That's going to leave a mark

SIMON WAS A SMART little mixed breed, black with a white patch on his chest. He loved to be walked. All dogs do. As a kid, one of my jobs was to take Simon to do his business.

On our strolls through the neighborhood, Simon and I passed nice houses with tidy lawns that had been manicured by elderly Italian men. These small patches of grass had been sweated and fretted over. Each blade was uniformly cut, the borders were neatly trimmed—they seemed flawless.

Simon, however, always felt something was amiss. The solution was quick at hand, or at paw. He would bound up to the nearest bush and lift his rear leg. A short tinkle later, all was right with the world. Simon had made his mark. This action was repeated house after house, all the way down the block.

I happened to recall these walks with Simon just before a meeting with Weyerhaeuser, the forest products giant. On that morning I was to present a new corporate brochure to their largest division. As odd as it sounds, a brochure can draw more scrutiny than a television campaign. Today's presentation had drawn a crowd; the room was filled with clients.

"Good morning," I began and then retold the story about my walks with Simon. As I concluded my remarks, more than one face wore a puzzled look.

I continued, "The reason I'm sharing this story with you is because at some point this morning you will know exactly how Simon felt. You will look at a sentence and feel compelled to add a comma. You will be gripped by the overwhelming need to change the word 'a' to the word 'the.' These types of changes, gentlemen, are marks." I paused to a few smiles and nods.

"On other occasions," I went on, "you will have real, meaningful changes to make. Please, speak up. Tell me what they are, and we will integrate them into the brochure. Your input is desired. It is needed to produce a piece that accurately reflects this division. However, I am asking you to edit yourself. A lot of people have worked very hard to create the piece that we will examine today. All I'm asking is that you don't piss all over it."

The room erupted in laughter. We worked very efficiently that morning with a high spirit of cooperation.

Marking isn't unique to advertising. We all have a little of Simon the dog in us. The overwhelming urge to tweak, adjust, clarify, tighten, sharpen or fine-tune exists wherever a pen is put to paper. Doctors, lawyers, MBAs, PhDs, clients, agencies, cops, criminals, birds and bees all do it.

Over time, I've come to see marking as the most powerful force in nature. To try to stop this behavior is folly. You have a better chance of stopping Hugh Grant from blinking.

So what's to be done? If you cannot prevent a behavior, you should try to turn it to your advantage. Expect your work to be marked by clients. Encourage it. That's actually what I was doing at the Weyerhaeuser meeting. Once the client marks your storyboard or print ad or landing page, he has put part of himself into the ad. It gives him a sense of ownership.

My old partner Ron Owens didn't look at marking as peeing on the ad. He always said that the client was sprinkling the ad with holy water, giving it his blessing. Either way, Ron's or Simon's, you get a little wet.

What's on the bottle is more important than what's in the bottle

SELLING PERFUME IS LIKE selling snake oil. Splash on this magic elixir, and suddenly you'll be attractive and desired. You will be transformed into Heidi Klum or Claudia Schiffer. Plunk down your money and change your life.

Put the same perfume in two different bottles, and you can sell it for two different prices. Selling perfume is as close to pure advertising as you can get. What's on the bottle is more important than what's in the bottle.

I cut my advertising teeth selling fragrance. That's if you consider Jovan to be fragrant. We were the Kmart of the fashion world. The products had names like Musk Oil, Sport Scent, Man, Woman and Sex Appeal. Subtle stuff like that.

The company had been started by a guy named Bernie Mitchell. When he decided to enter the perfume business, he looked at the successful players in the market. Two of the biggest were Revlon and Avon. So he created the name Jovan.

We were grateful that he stopped following Charles Revson's lead with the name of his company. After all, Revson had named one of the most successful perfumes in history after himself, "Charlie." If Mitchell had followed suit, we would have been trying to sell a perfume called "Bernie."

Bernie Mitchell's company did well. Jovan became very profitable. They hired J. Walter Thompson as their advertising agency.

Jovan was a fun account to work on. We were selling sex, plain and simple. That was great for me. As a twenty-five-year-old, I knew nothing of style, fashion or fragrance, but thanks to the generosity of women at the University of Connecticut, I knew about sex.

I was also learning about selling the benefits of a product rather than its features. This is a primary tenet of good advertising.

If you are describing a product, its smell, its taste, its ingredients, then you are talking about features.

If you are communicating how a product will make life better for the person who uses it, you are selling benefits.

Convincing someone that putting on a certain perfume will enhance their chances of having intimate relations with a member of the opposite sex is selling the benefit of that perfume. It's a better selling strategy than telling someone the perfume smells like jasmine.

Selling benefits works regardless of the product. Here's a story that Wally Armbruster told me. Wally ran the Budweiser account at D'Arcy McManus Masius in St. Louis for years. He had a long, successful career as an adman. The story is loosely paraphrased.

A man walks into a hardware store and asks to see the drill bits. The storeowner is quite proud of his extensive selection of bits and begins to describe the models he has for sale. One is made of titanium. Another has a special groove design. A third has a magnetic tip for holding screws. The owner wraps up his pitch by asking the customer, "Do you know which drill bit you want?"

"Oh, I don't really want a drill bit," the customer replied. "I want holes."

Advertisers ignore this lesson all the time. That's why you see ads that tout the speed of software, when you should be seeing ads that advertise finishing the job in half the time.

Pay heed. Customers buy benefits. Companies that advertise benefits will outsell those that advertise features.

While this observation seems self-evident, it's not. Highly trained advertising brand managers making six-figure salaries commonly ignore this obvious truth. They believe a large picture of their product on a magazine page will prove endlessly fascinating to the great American public. Sounds crazy, doesn't it? Perhaps this is the real reason we're called Mad Men.

As an unscrupulous adman, I have created and run ads that laud features rather than benefits. A person in my position can only recommend a course of action. When the client prefers a different course, putting up too much of a stink will brand you as an obstructionist. Such a person could be kicked off the account or even lose the account for the agency. So I do what I am told. You may perceive me as a spineless jellyfish, but I am an employed spineless jellyfish. This is why people in advertising drink so much.

The thing about perfume is that it doesn't have benefits. We had to create them out of thin air. This made Jovan the perfect incubator for my career. I was taught one of the most important lessons in advertising. One I use every day. Sell benefits not features.

Personally, I don't wear fragrance very often. I don't want to be transformed into Heidi Klum or Claudia Schiffer. Besides, I can't walk in heels.

Can you TIVO doomsday for me?

I WANTED TO TALK about TIVO before it becomes obsolete. Replaced by DVRs or whatever comes next.

A friend asked me if I felt that the invention of TIVO would put my job in jeopardy. Prior to him asking, I hadn't given it a thought. I turned the question around and asked how he heard about TIVO. You guessed it, he saw a television commercial.

When radio became popular in the early twentieth century, some felt it signaled the death of newspaper advertising. The new medium offered sound, rapt audiences and immediacy. There was no way newspapers could compete. They were doomed.

When television came along a few decades later, many felt the dollars would flow out of radio advertising into the new medium. On TV, advertisers could show their products, they could even give demonstrations. There was no way radio could compete with the exciting new visual medium. The radio advertising business was doomed, doomed I tell ya.

By the 1970s, the three networks had become saturated with ads. Television time was so expensive that the standard sixty-second TV spot had been replaced by the thirty-second spot. Fifteen-second commercials were gaining traction and even ten-second spots began to appear. Commercials had turned into little more than audiovisual billboards. The people who wrote commercials were doomed.

Then came cable. Suddenly, there was plenty of room for even hour-long infomercials. But what was good news for copywriters was certainly bad news for the networks. Cable let brand managers find niche audiences that matched their product's demographic very cost effectively. Broadcasting had given way to narrow casting. The networks were doomed!

Almost simultaneously, videocassette machines and tapes showed up. Many thought this would end television as we knew it and doom the advertising industry. Soon enough, videotapes, and later laser discs, began to arrive with advertising on them.

Then TIVO arrived. It could simply wipe out commercials. Finally, the advertising industry would bite the dust.

To make things worse, the internet is threatening to replace television completely. Weird thing though: one of the most popular things on the internet is newspapers. Isn't that where we started?

Well, excuse me if I'm not all a-Twitter. As Mark Twain said, "The stories of my death are greatly exaggerated."

Just in case there is any confusion, advertising isn't going anywhere. Advertising abides. It is and will be part of your life until the sun expands past the orbit of the earth in five billion years. We adapt, adjust, change, evolve, mutate, transform and just plain endure. Kill us and we will return from the dead in the sequel. We're zombies.

Jason Voorhees has nothing on us. In fact, I know a media director who is trying to buy ad space on Jason's hockey mask. It's the perfect aperture for a machete company. And wouldn't Freddie Kruger be a superb pitchman for Lee Press-On Nails?

Advertisers are no longer content to sponsor the programs. Once, we were happy to be the frame around the picture. Not anymore. Now we are demanding to be part of the show.

In the biz, it's called product placement. And it is a tsunami. Soon, viewers will be watching programs with more logos than a NASCAR fire suit.

Why should Scott Bakula drink a cup of coffee when he can enjoy a cup of Folgers? Better yet, shouldn't the entire cast of *NCIS: New Orleans* meet in Starbucks every morning? You think those oversized Coke cups on American Idol were bad? Just wait.

Believe you can escape to Netflix? Try counting the number of brand mentions next time you binge watch.

Product placement is a new arrow in our quiver, but the old arrows still shoot straight and true. Well, straight and true may not be the correct expression when we're talking about advertising, but you will get the point.

We will continue to bombard you with print, radio, television and internet ads. And prepare for lots of new stuff. In advertising circles we know what the plus in Google+ really stands for. It means Google plus a lot of ads.

There were ads in ancient Rome and in Shakespeare's London. Eventually, there will be ads on the moon. They might come through a smartphone or an Xbox or an iPad. I, for one, wouldn't be a bit surprised if they were delivered by a distant descendent of TIVO.

Advertising in an economic downturn

EVER HEAR OF MOXIE? Not many people have. At one time, it was the largest-selling soft drink in America.

So how did a brand that was bigger than Coca-Cola disappear from grocery shelves and consumer consciousness? It is an illuminating and cautionary tale for anyone who manages a brand.

The fact that Moxie ever achieved its lofty position is a story in itself. I've tried Moxie. Its flavor is awful, bitter with a strong aftertaste. I wanted to spit it out. Which begs a second question: how could such a terrible tasting drink have enjoyed so much success in the first place?

Both the rise and fall of Moxie can be attributed to advertising. The brand was one of the first to be introduced into the New York market. Being first, then and now, counts for a lot. Heavy advertising promoted Moxie. They had an early version of mobile billboards and a catchy jingle.

It worked. Being first, launching in the nation's largest market and having few viable competitors didn't hurt either.

Anyway, Moxie was out there kicking butt UNTIL . . . the great sugar shortage of 1919. Suddenly, one of the main ingredients in its formula leapt in price. Fearing higher prices, and to ensure the steady production of their soft drink, the company purchased huge amounts of sugar.

In many ways this is not unlike what happened with oil in 2008. That summer, the cost of oil went through the roof, soaring as high as $142 a barrel. Some companies, in an effort to stabilize their price for oil and to ensure their supply for the following winter, locked in the price at that very high number.

Unfortunately for oil buyers in 2008 and sugar buyers in 1919, the prices fell as quickly as they rose. Companies that had locked in the higher prices had locked out higher profits. To improve the balance sheet, Moxie decided to make some cuts. They cut—don't do it—their advertising budget.

The results were swift and dramatic. Sales plummeted. But the company managed to survive and, after resuming advertising, was soon flourishing again.

One might assume that this adventure, or more accurately, non–ad-venture, taught the folks at Moxie the importance of marketing. In this case, one would be wrong.

A decade later, the stock market crash began the Great Depression. Budgets were squeezed. Companies had to make tough decisions.

Moxie once again cut its ad budget. You know who kept advertising through those very lean years? Coca-Cola. And by the end of the Great Depression, Coke had emerged as the No. 1 selling soft drink in America.

Moxie didn't die. It survives to this day. You can still occasionally stumble across a dust-covered bottle sitting on a shelf. Anti-climactically, in 2005 Moxie became the Official Soft Drink of Maine. I am not joking.

Meanwhile, back on planet Earth, the economy continues its cycle of expansion and recession. Companies grow and shrink. And somewhere, out there in the advertising universe, an ad budget is coming under scrutiny. Hopefully someone in the room has heard of Moxie.

J. Walter after dark

As a young copywriter, I used to wander the halls of J. Walter Thompson at night looking for lighted offices. Lights meant two things, someone working late and alcohol. I wanted to find both.

People who are toiling into the evening will accept help from anybody, even a junior writer. In this way I got to work on almost every account in the agency. These nocturnal treks built my portfolio. The first ads I ever had produced were a series of small space newspaper ads for 7•UP. I wasn't assigned to 7•UP at the time. Prowling the corridors after hours provided the opportunity.

Some nights, I would stumble across bull sessions. These sessions were usually propelled by alcohol. I would come in and ask if the participants were working late and if they needed help. This Good Samaritan gesture would be responded to with an invitation to join the group and have a beer. I would respond in the affirmative.

Occasionally, substances slightly less legal than alcohol were being consumed. I would respond affirmatively in those cases as well.

One such occasion took a twist that had me rethinking my chosen occupation. A small group had congregated in a group creative director's corner office. This was a big break. Getting in the good graces of a creative director was a wise career move.

I walked into the office and asked, "Do you guys need any help?" The not-so-subtle odor of marijuana had already given the answer. "Not really." The great man said, "C'mon in."

Along with the creative director, an art director and a senior writer were in the office. There was also a bottle of Jameson on the desk. "Want a drink?"

"Sure." I replied. I've never been a big whiskey drinker, but this was too good to pass up. Sitting around with some senior guys getting a little drunk was heady stuff.

"Want something to smoke?" the art director asked, lifting his hand from the side of his chair revealing a smoking joint.

"Sure," I replied, and everyone laughed. This was really great. Drinking and smoking with a group creative director and a couple of his aces.

You have to remember that this was a different time. The year was 1977. Three-martini lunches were still pretty common. Roger Sterling would have fit nicely into the culture of JWT. The work environment was looser, easier. Thompson had a couple of secretaries who regularly wore see-through blouses to work. They didn't give it a second thought. I did. I thought about it a lot. Drugs were common and consumed fairly openly. And not just pot.

The problem was that I don't really like pot. It makes me paranoid. Still, I was fully confident that I could smoke and still come off as a relatively clever guy. It would just take some concentration. In no time, I had fit right in. We were having a grand old time.

Suddenly, the group creative director became serious. "I want to show you something," he said. "Look at this." We all drew in close to his desk. He picked up a reprint of a Gerber Baby Food ad that his group had done. The ad featured a soft-focus photograph of a newborn baby. It made you feel warm and fuzzy. In delicate type just above the infant's tiny hand the headline whispered, "Thursday, 3:32 a.m., a miracle named Jody."

Next he picked up a pad of tracing paper and ripped out a sheet. He placed the transparent paper over the ad and grabbed a pencil. With a few strokes he added a slight wisp of hair dropping over Jody's forehead. Under the baby's nose he drew a short square mustache.

Beautiful baby Jody was now the spitting image of Adolf Hitler. It was completely unnerving to look at. The incongruity of this tiny precious innocent being overlaid by a mask of pure evil was overwhelming. I was horrified, stunned, appalled. I didn't know what to say or how to act.

The others had no such indecision. "That's great!" roared the art director. They all laughed and nodded and seemed very pleased.

"Dave, do you like it?" I was asked. My answer wasn't forthcoming. I thought the whole thing was sick. But I did not want to offend a great and powerful group creative director, or maybe I should call him my Führer.

My confusion must have been apparent. "It's for Twentieth Century Fox," said the writer. "It's a movie poster." He went on to explain that the Los Angeles office had asked for help developing concepts for a new movie. The film was about cloning Adolf Hitler.

"Oooohh," I said, the light slowly illuminating my brain. It's a movie poster. These guys aren't really a bunch of Nazis. Whew, it's just a poster.

Slowly I regained the ability to form words. "It's great. Really eerie." I laughed and nodded and acted very pleased. The party broke up a short time later.

Once again I was in the darkened halls of J. Walter Thompson. Ahead, another lighted doorway beckoned. This time I walked straight back to my office, grabbed my coat, and headed into the cold, crisp Chicago night.

How did I get here anyhow?

IT's ODD THAT I have a career in advertising at all. I majored in Child Development and Family Relations in college, earning a Bachelor of Science in Home Economics. Yeah, that's right, Home Economics. You got a problem with that? I know it's a curious major for a man, the result of taking all the same courses as my girlfriend.

In college, I didn't even know that there were people who wrote ads for a living. Nor did I care. What I truly wanted was to become a stand-up comic. So I moved to Chicago after graduation and studied improvisation at Second City. That experiment ended when it was discovered that I wasn't very funny.

Another Second City aspirant became my friend. John McKee worked in advertising at J. Walter and introduced me to the business. We both got something out of the classes. I found a new career. John found a wife. If you ever met Cathy, he came out ahead on that one.

John helped me put together a portfolio of spec work. "Spec" is short for speculative or pretend ads put together to show prospective employers your writing skills. In advertising, a portfolio is also called a book. Today, young copywriters just post spec to a website. It comes to the same thing.

My first few tries were serious and self-conscious. John suggested I loosen up and use my sense of humor. Eventually, I crafted a lighthearted letter of introduction. It went like this:

Dear Sir,

As a young man, comedian Jerry Lewis sold a large quantity of stock to back a play. The play flopped. The stock was Polaroid. The following year, Mr. Lewis was offered the chance to back another play. He declined. That play was "My Fair Lady."

Recently Mr. Lewis invested 1.5 million dollars in a stage show called "Hellzapoppin." It flopped. Jerry Lewis has never sought out Dave Marinaccio for employment.

CAN HISTORY BE WRONG?

The letter went on to tell what a wonderful guy I was. I also included a resume along with the fake ads in my portfolio, which I might point out wasn't an actual portfolio but a letter-sized manila folder.

My first interview occurred at the forerunner of DDB Needham, Needham Harper & Steers. Their employees nick-named it Needlessly Harboring Fears. Needham was a top-notch agency that handled the McDonald's business.

I met with screener Jack Heatherington. He liked my book and sent me to a writer. The writer liked my stuff and sent me up the chain to associate creative director Peter Hale. Peter liked my portfolio and sent me to the creative director, Neil Vanover.

All in all, things were going swimmingly. Vanover took his time examining my work. Slowly he lifted his eyes toward me. I straightened. He spoke. "The first thing that strikes me is your resume." Holding the cleanly typed sheet in the air, he turned it over and slapped it down on his desk, blank side up. "This," he pronounced, "would be a better resume."

I gulped. Vanover proceeded to tell me that he was unim-pressed. Further, who was I to make fun of a beloved and respected personality like Jerry Lewis? I was faced with a contingency for which I hadn't planned. This guy was a Jerry Lewis fan.

J. Walter Thompson was the next agency to grant me an interview. After I met with Bob Jones, the creative director responsible for the Oscar Mayer account, he hired me.

My first week in advertising, I learned a lesson that has lasted the rest of my life. Previous to my employment by JWT, I had been working at the Howe Development Center as a mental health specialist for the state of Illinois. Across the street was a bowling alley. Every day at 5:01 p.m. the bowling alley bar would fill with state employees.

The bar would empty about thirty minutes after happy hour ended. I was usually still there. As folks came and went, they would toss their money on the table. By the end of the night, a pile of cash would have amassed.

Over time I had learned that the bill and tip would be easily paid from that pile with a few bucks left over. Sometimes there was enough to cover my portion of the tab. To drink free, all I had to do was drink long. Since I never had much money or anywhere to go, this fit my pocketbook and schedule perfectly.

At the end my first week at Thompson, I was invited to happy hour at the Embers. This was not like the bowling alley. It was swanky and dark. One of my coworkers played the piano while another sang. People in expensive suits populated the lounge. Drinks were poured with a heavy hand, while "Scotch and Soda" was sultrily styled in the background.

As the night wore on, a thought occurred to me. If I stuck around here, the pile of cash would be truly monumental. Of course, there wasn't a pile of cash at the Embers. People would just hand a couple of bills to those remaining behind. Ultimately, I was the sole survivor and the possessor of close to a hundred dollars.

When the waitress arrived with the check, I learned the difference between advertising and the Department of Mental Health. I was short thirty bucks.

All these suits and ties had stiffed each other. Some of these guys made eight or nine times the salary of a state employee. But they didn't even cover the cost of their own drinks. The guy holding the cash was also left holding the bag. Settling up with my credit card, a wiser man exited the Embers onto Oak Avenue.

Young graduates today miss that lesson. The road to advertising rarely detours through the Department of Mental Health. Every college with over a few hundred students offers advertising classes. I encounter these freshly scrubbed kids and their freshly scrubbed portfolios sitting on the other side of my desk.

They show me their class work. Make-believe ads prettified on a computer. Most of the products featured in these imaginary ads are the same: Crayola Crayons, Curaids, Nike, Mercedes and Sea-Doo, with a smidgen of public service advertising thrown in, usually about AIDS.

These products have one thing in common. They are inherently exciting. Just once I would love to see one of these kids take a crack at writing an ad for a boring product like a dishwasher. Like the man said, it's easy to write a love poem. It's difficult to write a love poem about a refrigerator. But that's advertising.

These monolithic portfolios are not really the kids' fault. Advertising instructors are the guiding force behind these indistinguishable efforts. They teach the kids the mistakes to avoid. This has the effect of homogenizing the books.

A newbie can only bring two things to an ad agency. One is a fresh perspective, a different way to look at things. Part of that is the ability to charge ahead and make an old mistake a brand new way. This is their best chance to show some original thinking.

The second quality is fun. We work long hours in this business. Nobody wants to work overtime with a junior who takes himself too seriously.

I think my silly Jerry Lewis letter showed both qualities. On the downside, it pissed a guy off. On the upside, Neil Vanover would have been an awful person for me to work under. I hope he and Jerry lived happily ever after.

What is an advertising agency?

LIKE MOST KIDS, I loved to fly around the neighborhood on my bike. The best place to really get going was hidden away in a patch of woods, a big gully with steep sides, a natural half-pipe. You could come roaring down one side and up the other.

One day, a friend of mine had a brainstorm. We could start our bikes on either side of the gully and come flying at each other. Then, just as we were about to hit, we could turn slightly, miss each other by inches and shoot up the opposite sides.

We both thought this was a terrific idea. To be especially safe, we decided ahead of time how to miss each other. He would turn left at the bottom of the hill, and I would turn right.

We didn't have the same style bikes. I had an imitation racing bike with razor thin wheels. My buddy had an old fashioned Schwinn with huge metal fenders covering big balloon tires. It probably weighed three times what my skinny little Italian knockoff weighed. I mention weight because of the role it plays in the equation for momentum.

A tiny flaw in our plan made the equation for momentum important. You may already be aware that when objects are moving toward each other that the left side of one is the right side of the other. We had put ourselves on a collision course. This realization came to me at the bottom of the gully as I turned directly into the path of my friend on his tank-like Schwinn. We smashed into each other with all the force our hairless preteen legs could muster.

My once sporty Italian-style racing bike resembled a balloon animal. Neither the Schwinn nor my friend had sustained any discernible damage. He had just plowed through me and continued on. Momentum!

I gathered up what was left of my bike and headed home wondering what had gone wrong. We had communicated perfectly. Our strategy was at fault.

And so it is in ad agencies. An agency needs more that the ability to craft a message. That message has to be on target. It has to produce the right result.

This is my wobbly way of introducing the concepts of organization and structure. Also, it occurs to me that if you are not in advertising, it would be good to talk about how an agency is structured.

Think of an ad agency as an architectural firm for marketing. We draw up blueprints for banners, brochures, landing pages, print ads and television commercials. Then we hire outsiders to do the work. Just as architects draw up plans and then hire a construction company to put up the steel and lay the brick.

For a television commercial, the blueprint is called a storyboard. After the client approves the storyboard, we hire a film production company and a director to shoot the spot. The film production company assembles cameramen, grips, gaffers, the crew who do the actual physical labor. We also hire composers to write the music and to hire musicians to play it. Voice-over is read by an announcer. An editor at a postproduction house is hired to put it all together.

Like architectural drawings, the advertising blueprint can change during production. Sometimes for the better, sometimes for worse. During production, it is the agency's job to stand around and drink coffee.

The blueprint for a print ad is called a layout. A photographer will be hired to shoot it. A printer will be hired print it. Look, ma, no hands.

The same is pretty much true for internet postings, with the difference being graphic artists take it to finish.

To accomplish these tasks, agencies are usually divided into the following departments: administrative, traffic, media, social media, research, account service, direct response, production and creative. Sometimes there are fewer departments.

A current oddity is some agencies have a department called digital. But these days everything is digital. Newspapers are digital. The reception desk is digital. Film cameras have been replaced by digital visual information capture. Digital media is just media. The term is so ubiquitous, it has no meaning. My cat Jerry is digital. Seriously, he has a digital chip in his neck that contains all the info needed to get him home if he is lost.

Yet, there are agencies that call themselves digital agencies, which basically means they do less. We have found digital elements slot easily into our existing structure.

Administrative is the same as in any other biz. They manage the finances, IT and general services. At most agencies, they make sure that an attractive receptionist greets you in the lobby.

The media department purchases the empty spaces and vacant time slots that will be filled with messaging. To do this, media controls most of the money in advertising. On a ten million dollar account, the media department will control nine million bucks.

Magazine space reps, television time salesmen and an army of people from Google vigorously vie for the attention of media planners and buyers. They ply them with tickets to every cool event, invite them to great parties and take them to lunch at the hottest, most expensive restaurants. If any of the remnants of Mad Men still exist, they are in the media department.

Research departments are usually small and unimportant. They rarely rise to the standards used in the academic world. Disaster checks are their primary concern.

Focus groups are the main component of advertising inquiry. If you have never been to a focus group, it is a small group of consumers who sit around a table and argue. This method of research is based on an Italian family at dinner minus the swearing in Italian. The conversation is analyzed and used to create messaging. I will get more deeply into this later in the book.

Account management is the liaison between the agency and the client. Account executives are also known as suits or AEs. They don't like to be called suits. Some of them like to be called project managers. Good AEs are advertising strategists and superb salesmen. Bad ones are indistinguishable from waiters, taking orders from clients and bringing them back to the kitchen.

Creative is the heart of an agency. It is where the ideas are created. This is where I work. We draw the blueprints. Writers and art directors move images on computer screens to create the ads and commercials that an agency produces. Narcissistically speaking, the other departments function as a life support system for the creative department.

Administrative, media, research or account service folks might have a different take on the structure of an agency. They can explain it in their books.

I could go on, but you get the basic idea. Anyway, once you've Frankensteined these pieces together, stick them in a high-rise on Madison Avenue, Michigan Avenue or Wilson Boulevard in Arlington, Virginia, and you've got yourself an ad agency. A collective of brilliance capable of creating the Maytag repairman or Ronald McDonald.

Do you really want to know what an advertising agency is? It is the totality of the minds of the people who work there. That's it. Period. The end.

Responding to a recent trend in advertising, agencies have taken to calling themselves communications companies. Communications companies act exactly the same as advertising agencies and are structured the same way. But now, they are communications companies. Get it?

In order to purvey the myth that they are now completely different, there are some new job titles. Account supervisors are called marketing communications managers or manager of marketing communications or communications manager. Notice the use of the word *communications*. Sometimes the word *strategic* or *brand* is used. Pretty cool, huh?

Regardless, they swim like a duck, walk like a duck and quack like a duck. And they still belong to the American Association of Advertising Agencies. Communications companies and brand agencies may call themselves something different. But exactly like, "You go left and I'll go right," they end up in exactly the same place.

What is a brand?

THERE IS A MISPERCEPTION that advertising creates brands. Brands exist independent of marketing. A brand is the sum total of everything that a customer thinks, feels, says and does pertaining to your product.

Forget products. <u>You</u> are a brand. Everything you do shapes opinions of you. Remember that time you puked at the party? Everyone at the party does.

Your clothes are your packaging. Are you a premium or a bargain basement brand? It doesn't matter if you care about it or not. There it is.

Here's the good part. Since brand is a perception, you can influence, to some degree, sometimes to a major degree, the perception.

One way is to spend bushels of money on advertising. Just flat out tell people what they should think. Then just keep telling 'em. Do this consistently over a long period of time, and lots of folks will accept it.

Kurt Vonnegut said, "You are what you pretend to be." And with enough money and consistency, there is some truth to that. However, branding functions best when there is honesty in the message. "A Diamond is Forever" is one of the truly great branding campaigns in history. It plays on a basic truth that diamonds are one of the hardest substances on the planet. They are forever. De Beers tied this premise to the aspirational. By giving a diamond to someone you love, it says your love is forever.

This campaign is more brilliant than any diamond could ever be. How do you think about diamonds? This campaign is probably why.

Often the way people interact with brands has nothing to do with ads. If your mother was run over by a guy in a Toyota, that association probably makes you invulnerable to Camry TV spots. In fact, branding that runs counter to personal experience with a product induces dissonance or outright enmity.

On the other hand, depending on your relationship with your mother, it might engender fondness for the Japanese auto giant. That's an evil thought.

Amazingly, brand advertising can also be used to drive reality. In the 1980s, Ford introduced "Quality is Job 1." At the time, Ford did not produce a high quality product. Most advertisers in that position would never have run that campaign. The conventional wisdom would dictate waiting until quality was improved to make such a statement.

But someone very smart at Ford decided to put the cart before the horse. They realized that such a campaign would drive quality. It let every worker on the assembly line know that excellence was their priority. It advised every manager at Ford how their decision-making should be based. To consumers it was a performance promise.

It worked. By the 1990s Ford was building a product that lived up to their tagline. Ford's TGW (Things Gone Wrong) numbers improved dramatically. The company was transformed.

No question, there were many internal changes at Ford. But I do not believe they would have worked as well without the boldness of going public with "Quality is Job 1." I consider this one of the best adverting campaigns in history, yet it rarely gets the accolades it deserves.

One thing deserves to be noted. Brand specialists or brand consultants did not create these great campaigns. The vast, vast majority of great campaigns were created by bright marketing directors working in concert with their ad agencies.

Consider, the only thing an agency does all day long is think about your brand. And they do it in real time, hands dirty, how does this work, from every angle, every single day. Nobody knows your brand better. Nobody could.

I'm not saying brand specialists have no place. They can help. But check with your agency first. And last. And listen to them.

So what is a brand? You tell me. It's what you think.

Do you know Dick?

ONE OF THE GREAT and horrible parts of working on Jovan was the opportunity to work with one of the biggest dicks I've ever met, Dick Meyer. Meyer stood six feet seven inches tall. He used every millimeter to intimidate.

Dick was the president of the company. He had a reputation for browbeating the agency—a reputation he had decidedly earned. Mercifully, most of his fits were aimed at my boss. Most, not all.

Even when he was being nice, he would still let you know that he was the big, rich, successful client. I recall one particular meeting where he plopped his angular frame into the chair next to mine. Out of the sleeve of his suit peeked a crimson sweater. The initials R. E. M. were monogrammed onto the sleeve.

"Touch it," he commanded. "Feel the material." I did. It felt soft and very expensive. Dick looked at me and smiled wryly.

"It's Cash Meyer," he said, his pronunciation lilting enough to let me know the sweater was cashmere. What a Dick.

For all of his faults, he did have a characteristic that should be transplanted into every client on Earth. He could make a decision.

This seems like a simple virtue. Normal humans make hundreds of decisions a day. Advertising humans, on the other hand, analyze, overanalyze, then second-, third- and fourth-guess every decision. If I had a penny for every time I heard someone say, "Let me play the devil's advocate," I would be a copper baron.

Dick never bothered with any of that. He made the call. He moved on, often mistaken but never uncertain.

From an agency point of view, this had many advantages. The major one being that we didn't have fifty rounds of revisions once Dick made up his mind.

Over the years, I've come to revere this ability. Many clients are simply incapable of making a decision. Seriously, I've walked into many a meeting knowing full well that we were not going to sell a blessed thing.

I once spent six months of my life working on a logo for an Atlanta radio station owned by a timid little man. We presented dozens of terrific logos, all of which were better than the one that the station was using. Eventually, the station owner overcame his fear and made a decision. He sold the station. The new owner changed the call letters and the advertising agency. Sheesh.

There are some clients who have no problem making a decision and then reversing it a day later. One day you come out of a meeting feeling great; the next you're back to square one.

Then there are the research junkies. Everything is pre-tested, post-tested, run through focus groups, backed by mall intercepts and scrubbed clean. If testing doesn't produce a clear winner, you start the process again. Rinse and repeat.

Sometimes the info doesn't help you make a decision. It's just testing gone wild. One of my favorite studies showed the different ways that consumers used toilet paper. Three distinct segments emerged: folders, rollers and scrunchers. Fascinating, no? Which are you?

Thank goodness the results of this useless information will never be used in a commercial. Can you imagine the spot that would result? Packaged goods companies like Procter & Gamble are notorious for this type of testing.

By far the strangest decision-making process I've encountered was used by Sunkist Orange Soda. Here's how it worked. The agency would present the advertising, and then everyone in the room would vote on their favorite ad. The ad with the most votes would be produced.

What truly made this process bizarre is that everyone's vote counted exactly the same. A junior copywriter's vote counted as much as the vote of the marketing director or the president of the company.

Once the agency figured that out, we would stuff the meeting with as many staffers as possible. Prior to the meeting, they would be given instructions on which ad should receive their votes.

To prevent us from stacking the deck, the client started holding meetings at their offices in Atlanta. The agency's offices were in Chicago. This made it expensive for the agency to put a lot of folks in the room.

As wacky as it was, this system produced decisions. We sold ads. We produced ads. We ran ads. And Sunkist sold the heck out of orange soda. Sunkist became the No. 1 orange soda in the country.

I've come to believe that any process that results in a decision is a good thing. Any process—whether it's voting, testing, coin flipping—it doesn't matter. If it produces a decision, it's a great way to go. The most important thing is to make a decision.

You know why? Because advertising works. Is that a self-serving statement? Do the Whalers belong in Hartford?

It works because any competent agency will give a client a number of solutions that will achieve the marketing objective at hand. Pick one. Pick any one. The worst thing you can do is overthink yourself into inactivity. While you're deciding, your competition is in the marketplace romancing consumers.

Truth be told, even bad advertising works. How many times have you looked at an ad or commercial you thought was stupid? How many times was that ad for a popular product? Think about it.

Dick never had a problem making a decision. In truth, even with all his posturing, I kinda liked Dick. He bought good work, and Jovan took home numerous awards. And when it came to making a decision, Dick didn't putz around.

Ethical advertising

ETHICAL ADVERTISING—NOW THERE'S an oxymoron. However, as a young idealist, my head was filled with such notions. Early in my career, I decided I would not work on cigarettes. Like Don Draper, a man must have a code of ethics. This was part of mine.

I held firm to that conviction until I discovered that Brown & Williamson Tobacco produced television commercials for foreign markets.

I would have forced my mother to smoke for the chance to do TV. Tobacco companies had big budgets. They used A-list directors. Ethics, shmethics, I jumped at the chance.

Writing advertising for foreign markets was a foreign experience. Day one I discovered I couldn't write anything clever. Puns and double entendres do not translate.

For example, when writing an ad for a low-tar cigarette you can't say, "Low-tar taste you can count on." The phrase *count on* doesn't have the same meaning in Arabic or Chinese as it does in English. It is not a synonym for *depend*, *rely* or *trust*. Its only meaning is "to enumerate in units." Therefore an Arab might think that you are asking him to use the cigarettes as a counting device.

One of the most famous examples of this type of miscommunication is from Pepsi. Their campaign slogan, "Come alive, you're in the Pepsi Generation" had an unintended meaning when translated into Chinese. It meant, loosely, "Pepsi brings your ancestors back from the dead." While that's a wonderful campaign promise, it caused some problems. That's the story, anyhow. I don't know if it's true.

So, as I said, my task on Brown & Williamson was to avoid writing anything clever. I did this exceptionally well.

Our meetings would take place in a conference room with the Brown & Williamson executives responsible for a particular brand. In the center of the table was a bowl filled with packs of cigarettes. Etiquette would dictate that you reach in the bowl, take out the appropriate pack, open it, tap out a cigarette and light up.

In no time at all, the room would fill with smoke. Your eyes would fill with tears. Your clothes would fill with smell, and the meeting would begin. When I hear people complain about secondhand smoke because some guy on a golf course, two fairways over, lit a cigar, I just wish I could teleport them into that room. You want secondhand smoke? I got your secondhand smoke right here.

Anyway, in addition to the language barrier, writing for foreign markets was strewn with cultural traps. Take the left hand. In certain countries, the left hand is considered the "dirty hand." Be careful how you use it in an ad. In other countries, putting either hand on a doorframe is thought to be impolite.

As a precaution, all our work had to be sent overseas to be checked before we could produce anything. Sometimes a piece would disappear for weeks before we heard anything. About the time we forgot the ad, we would get a request for a revision.

For the Brown & Williamson brand Kent, we worked with the Hong Kong office. I never met or even spoke to anyone from Hong Kong. I would attend a smoke-choked input meeting with the client and account guys, then write a spot.

Hong Kong asked that we create a sixty-second television commercial for Kent. The campaign had been well established. The tagline was simple, straightforward and not even remotely clever. "Fresh, calm, mild, Kent."

The existing foreign market Kent commercial featured a man on a beach, fishing with a net. He casts the net. He catches a fish. He lights up a Kent, inhales deeply, exhales orgasmically and stares at the sunset. Cut to a close-up of the pack as the singers croon, "Fresh, calm, mild, Kent."

This commercial was unacceptable to Hong Kong because, according to the Hong Kong office, the Chinese don't fish with nets.

We made a minor change. In our new version, the guy fished with a rod but everything else stayed the same. We packaged up the script and storyboard and sent them across the Pacific.

A few weeks later we received new information. According to the Hong Kong office, no one is ever alone in China. If a guy is alone on a beach he is a loser, an outcast, a man without friends.

So we rewrote the commercial to feature a couple of guys fishing with rods. They catch a fish. They both light up cigarettes, they inhale deeply, then exhale orgasmically and stare at the sunset. The singers come in, "Fresh, calm, mild, Kent."

Once again, the new scripts and storyboards made their way around the world for others to scrutinize.

After a few weeks, we once again received a request for a revision. Two guys were better than one, but the Chinese like to travel in groups. Could we enlarge the number of people involved? They also requested a little more action. Lose the fishing. Come up with something a little more active. Could you give the spot a little humor and fun?

Our answer to all these requests was yes. We were straying from the feeling of the slogan. None of this seemed fresh, calm or mild. But if it meant we could produce a television commercial, who cared?

Our next effort showed twenty people on the beach having a party. One of the guys climbs a coconut tree and tosses it down to the crowd. The coconut bounces off a guy's head and almost knocks him out. Everybody laughs, lights up cigarettes, inhales deeply, exhales orgasmically and the singers come in, "Fresh, calm, mild, Kent."

Three weeks later we get word that Hong Kong loved the coconut. But could we add something mechanical to the spot, like a motor scooter? Hell yes, we could. We'd come this far. A couple of fresh, calm, mild motor scooters coming right up!

So we rewrote the spot again. The new storyboard started with twenty motor scooters flying down the beach. Suddenly a coconut falls from a tree onto the head of the guy riding the lead scooter. He crashes causing a chain reaction pileup. Among the tangled arms, legs and scooters everyone lights up cigarettes. They inhale deeply, exhale orgasmically. Cue the singers. Fresh, calm, mild, Kent. Fresh, calm, mild, indeed.

The Hong Kong office loved it. They thanked us for the help and told us that they would produce the commercial themselves. They left us out in the cold. When we heard the news, we were neither fresh, nor calm, nor mild. Damn cigarette companies. Just ain't got no ethics.

While we're on the subject of ethics, I'd like to touch on one last thing about cigarette advertising. Not once in the years I worked on butts did anyone ever mention aiming ads at kids. It never came up. It was never discussed. Targeting never included anyone under eighteen years of age.

A few years later, Camel Cigarettes ran into trouble with their spokescamel, Joe. Interest groups were screaming that using an animated character to sell cigarettes proved that Camel was marketing to children.

Those same people probably also believe that the Jolly Green Giant was invented to sell frozen peas to children. The idea is ridiculous. I miss old Joe Camel, and I never believed for one second that he was intended to sell cigarettes to kids. In my opinion, he was a very ethical camel.

Make the logo bigger

I ALMOST CALLED THIS book Make the Logo Bigger. Everyone in the business has heard that phrase. Here's why.

Virtually every ad has a logo somewhere. The most common place to find one is in the lower right-hand corner of a print ad. Most television commercials save the last three seconds of a spot for the logo. There are no logos in radio. Duh.

Clients love logos. Actually, that's not quite right. Clients love their own logo. On the other hand, art directors tend to think of logos as tiny turds on their beautiful ads. They'll deny it if you ask, but it's true.

This sets up a classic battle that is repeated in conference rooms all over America. The agency brings in the ads. The client looks at the ads. The client looks in the lower right-hand corner of the ad and says, "The logo looks small." The agency art director defends the ad, saying, "If we make the logo any bigger it will distract from the ad."

The account guy will sense conflict and pretend he agrees with the art director while trying to placate the client. "What would you suggest, Mr. Client?" The universal client response is, "Make the logo bigger."

Sometimes the art director will make a last ditch effort to keep the logo small by saying, "If I make it any bigger it will look horsy." Art directors use words like *horsy* to describe anything they don't like.

This doesn't take into account that the client would love a logo as big as a horse. In fact, if you presented an ad with a logo as large as a horse, the client would say, "The logo looks small. Can we make it as big as an elephant?"

I've seen this scenario play out in countless meetings. Sometimes the client is more direct. Like at a Mazda meeting that a friend attended. I believe he quoted the client as saying, "Caw bigga, Mazda bigga, no dascussion I client."

Personally, I've made peace with logos. Big, small, medium-sized, I don't care. If it makes the client happy to have a horsy logo, let's saddle up and move on. The real problem isn't size, it's that companies often take their logos too seriously.

Say whaaa? Let me explain. Most logos are produced by design firms. To them a logo is a sacred cow. It cannot be touched or manipulated except in specially approved ways. These rules and regulations are written in a "bible" called a graphic standards manual. If you change the color of your logo, print it upside down or place it too close to another element in an ad, you are "violating" the logo.

According to these logo acolytes, if you violate these canons you will lose your trademark. Even worse, they warn that you will lose your identity. This is the biggest load of crap in advertising.

The real reason a great big book of rules and regulations accompanies a logo is to justify its enormous cost. If the firm that designed the logo showed up with only the logo, the client would jump out of his chair and scream, "I paid two hundred thousand dollars for that!?!" The big book calms them down.

The magnitude of this silliness is illustrated by the development of the NBC logo. More than a few years back, NBC paid $700,000 for a new logo. Soon after the logo was created, a problem occurred. A public television station in Nebraska had the exact same logo.

Okay, here's the interactive part of the book. How much did the Nebraska station pay for their logo—the one that was exactly the same as the NBC logo? Cut that number in half and guess. Sorry, it's still less than your guess. Ready? Less than $35.

That's right, thirty-five bucks. Now guess who got a bigger and better graphic standards manual? Bet you got that one right.

There are plenty of companies that treat their logos as sacrosanct. Great companies like Nike, Verizon and McDonald's. They all have one thing in common. Their logo is not responsible for their success.

That doesn't stop some extraordinary behavior. I had a client who pulled a tiny Pantone color chip from his wallet and held it up to a video monitor. The color chip matched the official color of his company's logo as mandated in the graphic standards manual. He wanted to check the color of his logo against the color of a company truck in his commercial. I didn't have the heart to tell him that he would need to go into every home and balance the color on every television set in the nation to match the colors perfectly.

His name was Dave. He was a pretty good client and a nice guy, but he was so caught up in the graphic standards manual that he went right off the deep end. Sorry, Dave.

Levi's, 7•UP and MTV have all built successful campaigns by manipulating, dare I say, violating their logos. Google monkeys with their logo almost every day. There are dozens of other examples.

If you are the brand manager of a company that is currently in logo development, I am going to save you hundreds of thousands of dollars. Here is Dave Marinaccio's down and dirty logo primer.

There are three types of logos: abstract, literal and iconic. Abstract logos are abstract shapes or designs that look good but don't mean much. Lucent Technologies has a beautiful red paintbrush circle as their logo. What does it mean? Beats me. It's abstract. It is also gone as the result of a merger. Nice logo, though.

IBM is a classic example of a literal logo. It is literally the letters I, B and M. Apple computer is a good example of an iconic logo, a representation of an apple with a bite out of it.

These different types of logos can be combined. You can have a literal icon or an abstract one. The aforementioned

Apple logo is a literal translation of their name but not of their business. Regardless, the three types of logos I've named basically cover everything out there.

So how do you judge a logo? What makes one good or bad? I use five criteria: Simple, Memorable, Distinctive Appropriate and Flexible.

Simple means simple. Don't junk it up with lots of words or images. A single strong graphic element usually works the best.

Memorable means, well, once you've seen the logo you recognize it.

Distinctive means that it doesn't look like other logos. It has a distinctive character, a uniqueness.

Appropriate means the logo should be suitable for the intended audiences and should not offend anyone that the logo is intended to influence. The Rolling Stones used a tongue sticking out of a huge pair of lips as a logo for a concert tour. Although some folks might have found the logo offensive, none of the target did. It was appropriate for the audiences they wanted to attract.

Flexible means a number of things. It refers to a logo's ability to work whether it is in color or in black and white. That it is equally recognizable large or small, on a billboard or business card. A flexible logo can be animated. It works in all media.

The marvelous thing about these criteria is that you don't need a design firm to explain them. Look at the logo. Is it simple, memorable, distinctive, appropriate and flexible? If your answer yes, you have a great logo. Is this the only system for judging a logo? I'm sure it's not. It's just a set of principles I have found useful.

You now have permission to throw your graphic standards manual away. I highly recommend it.

If you're a brand manager, go ahead, violate your logo, make it dance, let it sing, have it turn green and throw up. This will make someone in your legal department think you have given away your company's trademark. If so, sit down and talk, see if they have a point. Just use a little common sense, and, as Bob Marley said, "every little ting's gonna be all right."

Finally, make sure your agency makes the logo big enough. As you read this sentence, there is an art director in an office somewhere squeezing a logo into the tiniest possible space in the lower right-hand corner of an ad. Be gentle with him.

Killing days and buying days

MICHELLE PFEIFFER WASN'T BEAUTIFUL at nineteen. At least, not in the classically beautiful way she looks now. She was cute. Not yet a star, she was just another pretty Hollywood actress. I cast the nineteen-year-old Michelle in a commercial. We needed a young woman to play a beauty pageant contestant. Michelle was reigning Miss Orange County. Kismet.

I thought about asking her out. We had talked a little during the breaks in shooting. She was upbeat and fun. I didn't pull the trigger. It didn't seem like the right thing to do. Truth be told, I was probably a little intimidated. I feared a no.

No is probably the most used word in advertising. Writers hear it more often than a puppy does. Copywriters create hundreds of ads for every one or two that actually gets produced. The rest are rejected. No.

To thrive in this business you must make a friend of *no*. *No* means another opportunity. *No* is to be understood and accepted. *No* is the road to *yes*.

Let me take a brief diversion. When I moved to Atlanta to work at D'Arcy Masius Benton & Bowles, I discovered that Southerners rarely used the word *no*. Politeness is held in high esteem. *No* is very blunt.

One happy hour, an attractive young woman chanced to sit next to me at Clarence Fosters, my bistro of choice in this new city. She ordered with a heavy Southern accent, Carolinian as it turned out. I offered to buy the drink. She accepted. A pleasant conversation followed.

When her friends arrived, she didn't dash off to sit with them immediately. Instead she remained with me at the bar to finish the beverage I had purchased for her. I considered this a very good sign.

My next sentence was a proposition. "Would you like to have dinner sometime?" I queried.

"That's so sweet," she responded.

"Great," I said. "Pick any restaurant in the city."

"That's so sweet," she repeated.

"Is there any place special you want to go?" I thought I might have to suggest a restaurant.

"That's so sweet," she repeated again.

The third time was the charm. I understood. "That's so sweet," meant "NO." No, Dave, I do not want to go to dinner with you.

"Ooohhhh." I paused. I was tempted to say something tart, but she was so damn polite. "All right, well, have a nice time with your friends." I smiled. What the heck, I've had women say yes to me much less kindly. Welcome to the South.

It still comes down to *no*. In advertising you hear it every day, often for no good reason.

There is a concept in the ad business called killing days and buying days. Procter & Gamble are famous for it, but they don't hold a patent. All clients have them to some extent. If you have a presentation on a killing day, you won't sell a thing.

It doesn't matter what you present, they ain't buying. Your work has nothing to do with it. Sometimes the client is just in a foul mood. You picked the wrong day.

Buying days are the opposite. You're going to sell everything. You can do no wrong. You're in a zone! About the only negative is that you really have nothing to do with it. Whatever you present will be loved. The client is having a magnanimous day. Enjoy the experience.

Sounds crazy, no? Any long-term ad guy will have had the experience. A smart ad guy will cut his losses and get out of the room posthaste on a killing day. On a buying day, he'll press his luck and try to sell that network package everyone has been dreaming about. Reach for the stars, and you may get the moon.

It's easy to spot a killing day. But ego may prevent you from recognizing a buying day. After all, it's giving away the credit for a successful presentation. But who cares, they're buying!

And that's my regret when I remember my opportunity to ask out Michelle Pfeiffer. Maybe, just maybe, it might have been a buying day.

Influencers of purchase decision

I LEARNED THIS EARLY in my career, I don't recall where. I do recall that I never saw anyone use it. Heck, I never heard anyone even talk about it. Lots of agencies have some version of the graph I'm about to explain. I never saw any of them use it either.

Regardless, the think/feel diagram is the best advertising tool I've ever come across. I debated whether to share it in this book or not. Then I figured, even if I showed it to you, you wouldn't use it either. Fine. I still use it all the time.

Let's start with the influencers of purchase decision. There are only three. Your head, your heart and your habits.

We can get habits out of the way pretty quickly. Advertising almost never affects habits. They are formed in almost unconscious ways. If your mother bought a certain brand of soap, it's likely you will continue to buy that brand when you move away from mom. You do it automatically. Advertising can help break habits, but it cannot create habits.

That leaves your head, or rational thinking, and your heart, or emotions. The key is to understand how to use the head and heart.

This can be a little dry, so you might want to grab a glass of water.

Certain products are purchased based on rational decision making, thinking. Refrigerators are a good example. You look at the size, the price, the amount of energy it uses, freezer space and features like an in-door ice and water dispenser. Feelings play almost no role in purchasing a refrigerator.

Other products are purchased based on emotional appeal, feeling. Perfumes or jewelry fall into this category. You buy these products based on how they make you feel. Self-image plays a large role in the decision. Thinking is low priority in deciding this purchase.

Most products are a mix of thinking and feeling. Computers, clothes, beer, personal care products all have varying degrees of head and heart. The head/heart diagram I am about to describe shows advertisers how to craft a selling message to reach the appropriate influencer of purchase decision.

Still awake? This is very important, so stay with me.

Make a cross. At the top of the vertical line of the cross put the words *high head*. At the bottom of the vertical line put the words *low head*. To the right of the horizontal line put the words *high heart*. To the left of the horizontal line put the words *low heart*.

This is hard to visualize. Grab a pencil and draw the diagram, and it will become clear.

Once you have set up the diagram, products will fall easily onto this chart. Chewing gum will reside in the lower left-hand corner, as it is a low head, low heart product. Cars belong in the upper right-hand corner, as they must be sold using both the head and the heart.

Our old friend the refrigerator belongs in the upper left-hand corner. It is a high head, low heart product. You should now be able to draw your own chart and place any product on it. Where would you put a soft drink? Where would you put a diet soft drink?

This chart is a way to check if you are selling your product using the correct influencer of purchase. Here's the real payoff. If you can move any product on this chart toward the upper right-hand corner, consumers will pay more for it. And advertising can do that!

Example: if you can add an emotional element to the refrigerator, you move it closer to the upper right-hand corner and you can charge more for it. So let's make the fridge part of the Martha Stewart Collection. We'll add a patterned or textured surface and add a little circle with Martha's name near the handle. The result is a more valuable fridge.

But you don't even have to change the product; you can just introduce emotion into the advertising message. This will move the perception of your product toward the beckoning right-hand corner.

Apple computer does a very good job of this. Most decision points for buying a computer are rational. How much does it cost? How fast is it? How much RAM does it have? On our chart, computers would be well up the think line, almost to the top. On the feel line, computers fall near the middle or lower.

Apple advertising injects emotion into their product. There is no better example than the "Get a Mac" campaign. By using Justin Long as the personification of a Mac, they made their computer, which is nothing more than circuit boards in a box, charming, fun, irreverent and cool.

An often-unnoticed element of these commercials is the use of music. Music carries emotion without saying a word. The same image will be interpreted differently depending on the soundtrack, more on that later. In Apple's case, the light, up-lifting, music box score brings a pleasantness and affirmation to the Apple spots.

Together, Justin's natural charisma, the clever dialogue and the simple music create a feeling that purchasing a Mac reflects positively on one's self-image. It's a large step toward the upper right-hand corner of the chart and Apple reaps the rewards of that movement.

Apple has moved on from this campaign. I still consider it some of the best work they have done. Please note that in these ads Apple still addresses the primary product benefits of a computer. Much of the dialogue is devoted to the high head benefits of speed, processing and user friendliness. They did not abandon the primary benefits of their product in an attempt to move it to the golden upper right corner.

Once you understand the head/heart diagram, it will work for you. But only if, big if, you use it.

Zero tolerance

ONE OF MY FAVORITE *New Yorker* cartoons shows a large room filled with cubicles. Only a few of workers populate this expanse, giving the appearance of a ghost town. In the foreground two managers survey the sea of empty squares.

"Maybe zero tolerance is setting the bar too high."

Zero tolerance means absolute compliance with company rules. Any infraction is automatically punished by preset policy regardless of the individual circumstances of the transgression. No exceptions. As a company, we struggled with the idea of implementing a zero tolerance policy. We finally decided against it.

A lot of factors played into that decision. The most important was the creative culture of our shop. When exploring ways to position products, I want my writers and art directors to leave no stone unturned. To try new and un-expected things, I want them to push the boundaries.

One of the boundaries they inevitably come into contact with is the one between good taste and bad taste. This line isn't clear. It is a hazy shade of gray. How far you go in a beer commercial is much different from the line for a juice box ad. Different audiences have differing standards of what they will and won't accept.

A magazine page featuring a young man in his underwear with a large bulge in front is standard fare for Calvin Klein. Dress your model the same way for an Oscar Mayer Wiener ad and you will likely face a lawsuit. That doesn't mean a creative team working on hot dogs shouldn't occasionally play with such an idea. They probably should.

The line between good and bad taste is not only hazy, it moves. Over time, we have come to accept things that our parents would have found offensive. In the 1960s, the network censors had a rule that any scene that took place in a bedroom had to show separate beds. Today, such a rule seems foolish. But it is fair to assume that in the future folks will look back and find some of our mores just as foolish.

Advertising strives to be on the front edge of the curve. Get a little ahead of that curve, and zero tolerance gets you fired.

Truth be told, when writers and art directors cross the bounds of good taste, you can expect them to wallow in the mud for a while before they return. It ain't pretty. But it is necessary. Because if they don't go all the way to the line and over it, they will never know if they have gone far enough. We absolutely owe it to our clients to explore the outer limits.

If you walk by an office where one of these sessions is taking place, you might be offended. It offends me sometimes.

Don't misunderstand what I am saying. I am in no way condoning inappropriate or offensive behavior. If a person is offended, an immediate and sincere apology is called for. Sometimes sterner measures might be required.

What I am saying is that many of these transgressions are not personal. They are a hazard of working in advertising. If you take a job in asbestos removal, it's tough to complain that you don't want to be near asbestos.

If you choose to be in a creative environment of an ad agency, shit happens. Oops, see what I mean? Sorry.

For the above reasons, and a few more, we decided against zero tolerance. Personally, I've always felt that zero tolerance was an anti-intellectual position. It implies there are never extenuating circumstances that should be considered. That there is never an exception to the rule.

In my half century roaming around this planet, I've observed a truism about human beings. They are not perfect. Not a one of them. Why then, would we expect them to be perfect in the workplace?

Heck, there is no such thing as perfect. I remember the first time I looked through a loupe. A loupe is a small magnifying glass you can place on a surface and put one eye on. Jewelers use them to check gems. Art directors use them to check the printing on ads.

I picked up a loupe one day and put it over the logo of an ad. The magnification showed the straight edge of the logo to be extremely jagged. The perfectly straight line was an illusion.

Zero tolerance demands you fire a fine person who makes an innocent mistake. The standard and the price of such a policy are simply too high.

Worst of all, it eliminates one of the noblest of human qualities, forgiveness. Very often a second chance brings out the best in a person. You gain a better, more loyal employee than the one you had before the mistake.

And that is why I have zero tolerance for zero tolerance.

Clients get the advertising they deserve

ADVERTISING AGENCIES CLAIM THAT they are the crucial ingredient in the production of great advertising. Here's a dirty little secret. We're not. Most clients get the advertising they deserve.

Great advertising usually reflects more on the client than the agency. Take a great account like IKEA. When I worked on the account for the Swedish furniture manufacturer and outlet, we produced fun and creative ads. Give the same account to almost any agency in America, and wonderfully creative IKEA ads will suddenly start coming out of that shop.

On the other hand, take Gallo. Put that account in any agency in America, and drab, uninteresting ads will gush forth.

I worked only peripherally on Gallo. The account was in my creative group but handled by other teams. All their ads looked the same. Photography or film of a bottle of Gallo wine spiced with an occasional shot of a vineyard. It was boring, but it is exactly what the Gallo brothers wanted.

The only thing an agency can do is make recommendations. We can advise, suggest, cajole, even sit on the floor and beg like a dog, but we do not make the final decisions. If a client won't buy your good stuff, there ain't much you can do about it. It is their money, after all.

At a typical client meeting, an agency will present three ideas. The first is the idea everybody expects. It isn't that creative, but it isn't supposed to be. It is meant to communicate that you listened to the client's concerns and created a piece of advertising that responds directly to those concerns.

Idea #1 settles everyone down.

Idea #2 is more creative than #1. It is an unexpected solution to the marketing problem. You actually like it. It's a solid piece of work. Its major purpose is to open the thinking in the room.

Idea #3 is the one you want to sell. It's cool. When the entry forms for the award shows come around, this is the one you submit in multiple categories.

By the time you present idea #3, you're cooking. There is electricity in the room. The first two ideas were crude line drawings. Idea #3 uses photographs and computer type. To further tip the scales in your favor, you play a piece of music and read sample copy. All the stops have been pulled.

The last ad presented is virtually always the agency recommendation. I could walk into any agency/client meeting in the world. Heck, I could walk into a meeting where I didn't understand the language. I could sit. Watch the dog and pony show in Greek, Mongolian, Polynesian, whatever, then pick the best ad. It's the last one.

My underlying assumption in the previous scenario is that we're dealing with a competent and responsible agency. This is not always the case. There are a few less than responsible shops. If one of these is your agency, idea #3 is a flight of fancy. It won't sell squat. But these guys are few and far between. Bad agencies tend to die quick deaths, and the vast majority of shops do a good job.

So, a great client buys idea #3. A good client buys idea #2. A safe client buys idea #1.

And a bad client?

A bad client won't buy anything you create. They simply dictate the advertising to you. They tell you what to write, what to draw, then take the music home and ask their spouse's opinion.

I've written on accounts like that. They are no fun and the work usually sucks. In a situation like that, the best you can hope to do is save the client from himself. To take his or her ideas and polish them enough that they don't embarrass you or the agency.

Astonishingly, many bad and banal ideas work. Not because they are bad or banal, but because advertising works. Good advertising works better than bad advertising, but bad advertising works better than no advertising.

This often has the unfortunate effect of making the bad client believe he is a genius. Which means doing more crappy work with a smile. And as I've mentioned before, working on a crappy account is better than walking the streets looking for a job.

Let's recap. Good clients get good work. Bad clients get bad work. There are exceptions but fewer than you think. This produces a great dilemma in the advertising business. Many profitable accounts are very bad clients.

The dilemma is not whether agencies should pursue these profitable bad boys. The problem is how to delude ourselves into thinking we will change them into good accounts.

One of the great myths in advertising is that you can turn a bad client into a good client. The reason agencies believe this myth is twofold. First is the fact that all agencies hold to an unshakable belief that they are better than the shop down the street. That they have understanding and talent that no one else does. They believe they are special.

The second reason is M-O-N-E-Y. The more profitable an account, the greater the willingness there is to look past obvious flaws. Money blinds agencies to the fact that an account is terrible to work on.

Denial and greed are a potent combination. Guess how agencies solve the dilemma. Do we go after the bad client? Do they sell T-shirts at Venice Beach?

Alas, the agency will not change the bad client. More likely, the bad client will change the agency. But it will all come down to the same thing. The client will get exactly the work they deserve.

So, if you are a client, and you want to be a great client, what do you do? How can you inspire great, creative work?

Start with a well-written strategy brief. Take the word "brief" seriously. Shorter is better. This is not a brand statement, but a document focused narrowly on the task at hand. The more narrowly you define the goal, the greater the chance the agency will achieve it.

As you move to creative development, it is okay to dictate an idea, as long as your idea is a jumping-off point for the agency. In some ways giving the agency a first idea will get them headed in the right direction. Let the agency know you want the benefit of their thinking. Don't let your idea be the beginning and end of the process.

Tell the agency your true objective. I've mentioned this before. If you want the agency to succeed, they need to solve the right problem. Tell them the problem you need solved. Or if you're a glass half-full kind of guy, tell them where the opportunity lies.

Don't be impatient. Give the agency time and space to work. The right solution is always better than the quick solution. A week is a reasonable time frame to develop an internet banner. For an ad give 'em two weeks. Television requires a month.

When the work is presented, give the agency the benefit of the doubt. If they present something they believe in—and you don't—take a second and try to see their point of view.

Enjoy yourself. Every person at the agency wants to please you. Well, every sane person at the agency. That's a great chair to sit in. When the agency feels relaxed, it will be more forthcoming with ideas, both in quality and in quantity.

Simple, huh? Follow these steps and you'll be a better client. Which is in your best interest because your agency will become a better agency. And you know what? You'll deserve it.

What's in a nameplate?

MY FIRST OFFICE WAS a converted conference room. I use the word *converted* advisedly. My office would revert to its former life before my eyes as I sat at my desk. Without warning, much less my consent, guys would walk into my office and start a meeting.

This major inconvenience had an advantage. I got to know the inner workings of many accounts. I was like wallpaper. Senior executives would talk freely in front of me as if I wasn't there. Often I knew what was happening at the agency before many of my colleagues. Still, I wanted a real office.

When I got one, it also had an inconvenience. The new digs were right across the hall from the agency's main screening room. As the closest private space to the screening room, my office became a phone booth for agency clients.

Twice a day or more, I would return to my office and find the door shut. As a junior member of the firm, I couldn't bust in on an important client and kick him out. So I would wait patiently until the door opened and return to my desk. It sucked.

Necessity became the mother of invention, and I came up with, in all humility, a brilliant idea. I changed my nameplate. According to my new nameplate, which I altered using the same typeface as the others in the hall, I was no longer David Marinaccio. The resident of the office across from the screening room was now, "Dr. David Marinaccio, PhD."

It worked like a charm. Clients looking for private space now occupied Larry Butts's office just up the corridor from mine. I mean, whose office would you impose on, a PhD's or some guy named Butts's?

A critical part of the deception was using the exact typeface that adorned the other nameplates. Typefaces are an essential part of messaging. Type can change the meaning of a word. In advertising, it is often said that type talks. In fact, sometimes it screams.

Here are a couple of examples. Imagine you're driving down the road and see a vegetable stand. The sign out front is hand-painted on a piece of plywood. It says, "FRESH STRAWBERRIES."

Another mile down the road is a brick building. Its sign is highly polished and made out of metal. It says, "PRECISION ENGINEERING."

Yeah, so what? Well, let's switch the signs. In front of the brick building place a piece of plywood with hand-painted letters reading "PRECISION ENGINEERING." Would you have confidence in the ability of that company to deliver precision materials?

Conversely, a highly polished metal sign in front of the vegetable stand would convince few that the strawberries were picked that morning.

My little nameplate worked because it sent all the right signals. It was believable. I remained happily undisturbed in that office for the remainder of my tenure at JWT.

Eventually I moved on to a new job. Never again would I suffer the indignity of residence in a conference room or having my office used as a phone booth. But I wasn't taking any chances. One of my first acts was to create a nameplate that matched the others at my new company. It read "Dr. David Marinaccio, PhD."

Bewitched

My FIRST INTRODUCTION TO advertising was on television. I am not referring to the ads themselves. Darren Stevens, the husband of Samantha the witch on ABC sitcom *Bewitched*, worked at an ad agency. McMahon and Tate to be precise.

The entire agency consisted of Darren and his boss, Larry Tate. I don't believe we were ever shown another employee.

Of course, they didn't need anyone else. Darren was the creative department, account service and media all rolled into one tidy package. Mr. Tate's job consisted of taking the clients to lunch and yelling at Darren. For a long time, that was my only impression of the business.

That's how it pretty much remained until *Bosom Buddies* introduced the world to a twenty-four-year-old actor named Tom Hanks. Hanks and Peter Scolari played two poor creative admen who dressed as women so they could afford to live in a New York City apartment. You can reread that sentence if you like. Get the clever name of the show? This really was a prime-time series in the early eighties. I'm sure Hanks will be thrilled that I'm reminding folks.

Anyhow, Kip Wilson (Hanks) and Henry Desmond (Scolari) toiled at Livingston, Gentry and Miskin. As usual, advertising played a bit part. However, Hanks was an art director and Scolari a copywriter, the actual team concept used in the business. This was definitely a step up in reality from Darren Stevens. And there were even, gasp, other humans in the office.

For some reason, it took until the end of the decade for another prime-time series to be set in an ad agency. *Thirtysomething* took place in a small shop owned by writer Michael Steadman and art director Elliott Weston. The characters were excruciating angst-filled narcissists who thought, rethought and overthought every situation introduced in every episode.

By this time, I was actually in the business. Truth be told, this depiction of an agency was within the margin of error. Later, their shop was bought by a larger agency DAA. This rang true as well. The late eighties and early nineties were a time of merger mania in the real ad world.

Which brings us to *Mad Men*. *Mad Men* is set in the same time period as *Bewitched*. So theoretically, Don Draper could have been lured away by McMahon and Tate and worked with Darren Stevens. That would have been my dream ending to the series. Alas.

I must admit to liking *Mad Men*. Pretty much everyone in advertising does. It's stylish, well written and hits the cultural cues of the business pitch perfectly. And if advertising had a golden age, this was it.

It was a time when, on the spur of the moment, David Ogilvy put an eye patch on a shirt model and launched a phenomenon. Not unlike Draper walking into a meeting without an idea and producing one on the spot. In both cases, the client buys the idea and loves him for it. Bewitched, indeed.

Intelligence at play

A YOUNG WOMAN ONCE sat across my desk and tried to convince me to hire her because she had scored highly on a creativity test. Is there a greater oxymoron than a standardized test of creativity? Anyway, I didn't hire her.

The whole creativity thing in advertising is misunderstood. It's easy to see why. We call the department that makes the ads the Creative Department. The guy who runs the department is called the creative director. We use the word *creative* so often it seems like it's the only word we can think of. Not very imaginative, are we?

Vincent Van Gogh was wildly creative, a true original. He sold one painting in his life, to his brother. No one understood him. He would have been a disaster as an adman.

Great work walks a tightrope. It's creative enough to be interesting yet familiar, unusual yet accessible, both unexpected and relevant.

There are plenty of tremendously creative commercials that have been failures. One of my favorite spots was created for Nissan by ad genius Lee Clow. It featured a G.I. Joe–type soldier being held in the mouth of a toy T. rex. The soldier jumps out of the dinosaur's mouth, hops into a toy Nissan and tools down the corridor to a girl's bedroom, where he drives up to a dollhouse and picks up Barbie. A distraught Ken looks on from the balcony of the dollhouse as G.I. Joe drives off with Barbie in the Nissan. The spot was hilarious.

According to Lee, it didn't work. Viewers couldn't make the leap from the cool toy car to the real thing. A delightfully original and entertaining commercial didn't sell anything.

Meanwhile, Mr. Clean endures, successfully selling millions of units of cleaner by folding his arms and nodding his bald noggin. If you're looking for justice, pick another profession.

If creativity is intelligence at play, then advertising is creativity at work. It has to be harnessed.

In algebra class at Enfield High School, I learned a concept called least common denominator or LCD. In mathematics, LCD is the lowest (or smallest) number that can be divided evenly into a denominator (the number under the line in a fraction) LCD should be the goal of creativity in advertising. Find what is common to everyone in a larger group.

Effective ads have an element of universality. Finding that universality and presenting it in an interesting way is truly creative. If you can take common experiences and present them in an entertaining fashion, you will make an impression on folks and influence them to buy.

People have to be able to relate to an ad. If they can't, you won't sell a thing regardless of how wonderfully creative the approach.

Much of the advertising industry lives in denial of this fact. Writers and art directors are hired and promoted based on their perceived creativity. Award shows venerate the most outlandish executions without regard to their success at advertising's primary mission, sales. And newbies want jobs because they scored highly on a standardized test of creativity.

Hard softballs

In Chicago, they play softball with a sixteen-inch ball and no gloves. The rules specify that the same ball must be used for the entire game. By the third or fourth inning, the ball has been beaten to mush. In the first inning, however, it's as hard as a rock.

Chicago softball players are easily identifiable by their bent and twisted fingers. You can spot them another way. The names across the front of their jerseys are ad agencies.

I played a number of seasons in the Chicago Ad League. A tradition of sorts is that the opposing teams drink together after the game. In this way, the softball league acts as a conduit for making industry contacts, in many cases, drunken contacts. And if one is very lucky, drunken female contacts.

The league gives the Chicago ad community a center, perhaps even a soul. This is not to be underestimated in the world of advertising. The industry is rapidly becoming decentralized.

New York is still considered the heart of the industry but just barely. Good work comes from all over. Chicago and San Francisco produce comparable, often better, ads. Atlanta, Minneapolis, San Francisco and St. Louis all have great shops that do wonderful work, Austin, Boston, Richmond, DC, Portland, Seattle, Pittsburgh, Philly, too. I don't mean to leave anyone out.

The idea that one must search up and down Madison Avenue to find a great agency is an anachronism. With apologies to Sterling Cooper, you are as likely to find a great shop on lower Fifth or in Brooklyn.

The same is true of our suppliers. Excellent film companies, music houses and postproduction facilities are found all over the country. I once produced music tracks in Norman, Oklahoma. At first blush, I had little hope we could produce a quality product on the prairie. The studio was small. It was in an alley behind a hair salon. None of these things raises your confidence.

A brief conversation with the engineer convinced me that he knew his way around a recording board. After all, Pro Tools are Pro Tools. The musicians looked like musicians everywhere. Long hair, rough around the edges, with a slightly distracted air about them.

Moments into the first take, I realized these guys could play. The drummer was rock solid. The guitarist cooked. They were tight.

Why was I surprised? I've seen great bands in clubs in Des Moines, Springfield, Sacramento, Panama City, Bisbee, Fargo, Little Rock and New Haven. Every place I've been has its share of great musicians. I'm not suggesting that Norman would be a good spot to find an elite string section, but the tracks turned out great.

I expect the decentralization of the ad industry to continue. The internet makes it possible to hire freelance writers from all over the world and talk to them in real time.

That's what makes the Chicago Advertising Softball League so special. Large and small agencies, media planners, account guys and art directors all share a level playing field. They all share experiences like the one I'm about to describe.

We, JWT, were playing Leo Burnett. Their third baseman was a very obnoxious guy. He ran over our first baseman in the top of the first inning. Just plowed into him for no reason, a definite no-no.

In the bottom of the inning, an account guy, Ralph Kurak, singled to center. If the name sounds familiar, Ralph is a former Chicago Bear. He was the blocking back for Gayle Sayers, and his name is mentioned in the movie *Brian's Song*. He's a big guy.

I followed Ralph to the plate and lifted a fly to right field. As the right fielder caught the ball, Ralph tagged and ran to second. Ralph reached second base about the time the throw from the outfield reached the infield.

This didn't slow Ralph at all. He rounded the base and continued on. The ball was relayed to third and the third baseman was in possession of it by the time Ralph was only a few steps off second.

I thought Ralph would be out by a mile. Then I realized what was happening. Ralph was gaining speed. He looked like a locomotive. The third baseman, who was no doubt revisiting his decision to run over our first baseman, was frozen in fear as Ralph bore down on him.

The collision was out of a cartoon. A big rolling cloud of dust with arms and legs sticking out. Ralph and the obnoxious third baseman came to stop twenty feet past the base. As the dust settled, the ball slowly trickled away. Ralph got up and trotted home. The third baseman eventually got up and hobbled back to the bag.

This was one of my finest moments in advertising. It brought the team together in a way no other agency activity could. The story was told and retold over pitchers of beer that night. Surprisingly, a number of Leo Burnetters told us that they enjoyed seeing their obnoxious third baseman taught a lesson as much as we did.

The story made the rounds through the agency the next day. I can't prove we were a better agency for the experience. We sure felt more like a team. That's sometimes lacking in our biz.

I've played in other ad leagues but none that had the sense of community they have achieved in the Windy City. To this day, if I see an art director with gnarly fingers, I always ask, "You ever work in Chicago?"

Life is a contact sport

I WROTE THAT LINE for SportScents perfume and cologne in 1978. It was the first slogan I ever sold for a multimillion-dollar product launch. Soon after, the phrase began to pop up in the popular culture. A friend showed me a *Hagar the Horrible* comic strip that used it as a punch line. It still shows up now and again.

A couple of years ago I was sitting in the green room of a television studio on a book tour. Among the guests was another writer. He was promoting a book with the title *Life Is a Contact Sport.*

I was about to say, "Hey, I wrote the title to your book a couple of decades ago," before I caught myself. If the author took it the wrong way, it wouldn't have been in anyone's interest. I figured I would mention it after the show.

This sort of thing happens all the time. It isn't because people are stealing ideas. We live in the same environment. We get the same news. Watch the same famous people for entertainment. Eat in the same chain restaurants. Similar ideas, often identical ideas, occur to all of us.

For decades, the covers of *Time* and *Newsweek* were nearly identical on any given Monday. On any night Conan and Fallon are telling nearly the same jokes. Think they're spying on each other? Perhaps? It seems more likely that they live and work in the same culture and find the same stuff amusing.

In a first-round creative meeting, different copywriters will present the same idea. It is usually something mundane. Nonetheless, they all present it. They have to. If they leave out the idea because it's too obvious and that idea ends up as the campaign, they won't get any credit.

When I worked on Pizza Hut, everyone suggested using the song "At the Hop" by Danny and the Juniors. Everyone also suggested changing the words from "Let's go to the Hop" to "Let's go to the Hut."

I heard "Let's Go to the Hut" presented dozens of times. I also presented it myself as a preemptive strike in case it was chosen. No one stole this idea from anyone else. It was just obvious. I think, eventually, long after I left Foote Cone, they actually produced it. I wonder who got credit.

I mention this because some time in the future you will be watching TV and you will see a commercial you thought of. Nobody read your mind. You don't have to cover your head in tin foil. It just happens that way. Honestly.

I once developed an ad with an art director and later discovered virtually the same idea in a book of award-wining ads. When I told the art director of my discovery, he started to get upset. "I can understand why you're mad," I said. "It's a bitch when somebody steals your idea before you even have it."

I'm not saying that ad agencies don't steal ideas. We do. We steal from movies, from websites and from each other. If a rock star shows up on Monday wearing a tie-dye sombrero, expect to see on-camera pitchmen wearing tie-dye sombreros by the weekend, for sure by Tuesday.

One of my favorite knockoffs was done for a kids' drink called Sip Ups. When the client decided to start selling Sip Ups in Puerto Rico, the agency suggested using the kid supergroup Menudo as spokesmen, or more accurately, spokeskids. However, the agency was unable to work out an acceptable deal with the group's management.

Instead, an ad was produced using unknown youngsters the same age as the group in a rock concert setting. Internally, we referred to the band in the commercial as the pseudo Menudo.

I don't know if anyone had previously penned the phrase "Life is a contact sport" before I delivered it to the popular culture. It doesn't matter. What does matter is that SportScents was launched successfully and sold strongly for years. My job is to sell stuff.

I never said "Boo" to the guy who wrote the *Life is a Contact Sport* book. Until now.

What do you do for a living?

WHEN STRANGERS FIND OUT that you work in advertising, they almost invariably will tell you their ideas for commercials. I don't believe this happens in other occupations. When someone meets an architect, do they immediately launch into their idea for a bridge?

Listening to bad ideas for TV spots is preferable to the other topic of conversation that usually comes up. Could you cast their cute kid in a commercial? It doesn't matter if little Jason has eight eyes and two noses. He's model material.

A few of the spots I've been pitched have been pretty good. At some time or other nearly everybody will come up with a decent idea for a commercial. It's not that difficult. Most times my agency doesn't handle the product they're pitching but that never slows anyone down.

Writing commercials is like kicking extra points in a football game. Stay with me. When you watch a game, it's obvious that you could not be a lineman. Those guys are huge, with arms that are as big as your waist. The running backs are fast and elusive. The quarterback throws the ball seventy yards. Wide receivers leap in the air and catch passes while taking hits that would put most of us in the hospital. You absolutely know that you are incapable of any of those things.

But after a touchdown, a little guy comes out and kicks the extra point from the ten-yard line. He's only five feet nine inches tall and weighs 180 pounds. Hey, that's easy. You could do that. You could kick an extra point.

What you can't do is make every single extra point all season long with 300-pound defenders charging toward you, when rain is falling, the wind is swirling, 80,000 raucous fans are screaming and the game is hanging in the balance.

That's the difference between an ad and advertising. Anyone can write an ad. What they can't do is write an ad on deadline, on budget, with sales going down, the client all over your back, the phone ringing, and you need to have an idea, NOW. Then tomorrow, when everything you have done is rejected, resetting and delivering a fresh approach. And, of course, never missing an extra point.

I imagine every occupation comes with a cross to bear. Listening to a few bad ideas for commercials is not a crushing burden. The fact that folks are actually interested in my job reminds me that the ad biz is a pretty good gig. And I should be thankful that I don't actually have 300-pound defensive linemen running at me when I'm working on an email blast.

Triage

I SHOT, ON FILM, a National Guard field exercise in Springfield, Missouri. Helicopters were bringing in the wounded. Nurses and doctors were scampering around like an episode of *M*A*S*H*, which wasn't surprising because we were filming a MASH unit.

One of the very first procedures the unit performs upon receiving incoming casualties is to separate them into three groups. The first group has injuries that demand immediate medical attention to survive. The second group is made up of wounded who can wait to be treated. The third group consists of individuals beyond help. This sorting of patients is called triage.

These are difficult decisions to make, literally life and death. Advertising should not be confused with a life-and-death endeavor. We do, however, employ the practice of triage.

Most agencies will deny it. But intelligent creative directors perform triage every day.

In the first group are ads that are critical to the agency and the client. They are highly visible. Success or failure of these campaigns can affect sales or the client/agency relationship. Sometimes they are ads with immediate deadlines. Regardless of what else is in the shop, these guys move to the front of the line.

In the second group are ads that are important but are either routine or low profile. Even when this group has a tight timeline, they can wait.

Unlike actual triage, we can't put any ads to the side and just let them die, although we would like to for the third group. This is the necessary stuff no one wants to work on. The main priority for this group is to get 'em out of the agency on the path of least resistance. GITFO is a term often applied to these jobs. GITFO stands for "get it the freak out of here," or something very close to that.

A job from the third group can move into the second group if there is an unusual challenge or the chance to have fun with it. Because group three ads are under the radar, they can sometimes offer a bit of creative freedom. Mostly though, they fall to the bottom of the agency to be worked on by junior writers learning their craft.

Even admen who may be horrified that I have committed this truth to paper use this practice. It's absolutely necessary.

Without priorities, no manager could run a business. Any business.

Still, most agencies will tell clients that every job is important. I have heard the phrase, "There are no small jobs," spit out at meetings. That "We work as hard on an email subject line as we do on a television commercial." It's rhetoric.

What your agency owes you is to handle these low-priority jobs in a competent manner. To make sure they look and feel like they were produced by professionals. To bring them in on time and on budget. Then to traffic them out of the shop in an orderly and efficient manner.

Seriously, would you want your advertising agency to spend as much time on a matchbook cover as they do on your new national branding campaign? If you do, you're mentally ill. And so are the folks at your agency.

A great brand manager will perform triage before a job even gets to the ad agency. He will have set his priorities and his expectations.

Every good manager performs some manner of triage when we are faced with a decision. That is as true in our personal lives as it is in business. Time is not an infinite resource. You need to make choices.

I told you I would be honest in this book, and that's as honest as it gets. Yes, Virginia, sometimes agencies give certain jobs short shrift. We perform triage out of pragmatism, which is an excellent business practice.

And the award for the best award show goes to . . .

THE O'TOOLE AWARDS ARE the American Association of Advertising Agencies' (4As) annual creative awards. They are named after John O'Toole, long-time 4As president and well-known ad legend. Before John O'Toole was an award he was a creative director. A very good one, too. After all, he did have the good sense to hire me. That alone should secure his place in the Advertising Hall of Fame.

I must admit I have never won an O'Toole Award. That isn't shocking, because I have never entered the O'Toole Awards.

Before you get the wrong idea, I have won my fair share of certificates and statuettes. I've won ADDYs and Gold Awards and been recognized in *AdWeek's* Best Ads of the Year. I've also collected category awards by the score.

LMO does enter award shows. But we do it mostly for the kids, the young writers, art directors and designers who consider awards an imprimatur, a validation of their career choice.

I have a couple of problems with awards. Advertising awards exist to make money for the producers of advertising award shows. It's a business. If the owners of a given award show thought they could make more money with a competition for footwear, then the CLIO's would be presented to the designers of stiletto heels.

Further, the criteria for victory borders on the inane. You can win Best in Show for a commercial that drove your client out of business. It's true.

That's because most shows judge the work for its "creative" content. Ads that win are usually funny or entertaining. Whether the ad sold anything or not isn't even considered.

It's the equivalent of determining college admission by head size. It's not a meaningful predictor of performance. Well, it's not a meaningful predictor of academic performance.

That is not to say that advertising awards are without value. As noted, they are good for morale, especially among younger staffers. They look nice on a shelf in the agency lobby. Since many creative directors are egotistical enough to think they are important, they make an impressive couple of lines on a résumé. And, amazingly, there are even some clients who think this is an important measure of an agency.

The shows themselves can be fun, an aspect of an outing never to be underestimated. You run into folks you haven't seen in a while, former coworkers or clients. There is usually a little buzz. Folks are dressed up and look nice. There is alcohol.

Ultimately, though, the award shows are meaningless and vain. So how should we view John O'Toole's legacy? I'm satisfied with the fact that he was smart enough to hire me.

Hanging in there

LET ME TELL YOU about my honeymoon. The wedding was beautiful. A gorgeous day on a charming deck, above a glistening Long Island Sound, a handsome groom, a beautiful bride, wonderful family and friends. Nice wedding.

The next morning we were scheduled to fly to Jamaica with a connection in Miami. We were up before the break of dawn for a 6:45 a.m. departure. Arriving at the gate, I cast an eye out the window and saw a Boeing 727. A good sign, the plane was at the gate.

A bad sign quickly followed. Bright red letters on the message board behind the gate agents flashed DELAYED. This puppy wasn't going to take off until 7:30 a.m. Damn, if I'd known that, we could have slept another forty-five minutes.

Well, whaddya gonna do? Breakfast seemed like a good option. So we sought out sustenance, which also ate up enough time to return during boarding. Except it wasn't. Boarding, that is. The departure time had been moved back another hour.

The day that had started with such promise was now dragging our spirits down. Agonizingly, the moments ticked by. Each minute it became less likely that we would make our connection in Miami. If we ever got to Miami.

They changed the board again to alert us to the fact that the scheduled departure time was now noon. Another opportunity to drag our luggage to the airport cafeteria.

By this time, we knew most of the other passengers quite well. Early on, folks went to the counter, got some tiny piece of information and returned to their seats. But after five hours in the waiting area, we had become an efficient community. We traded every scrap of information, every overheard conversation. Slowly, without any help from American Airlines, bit by bit, we, the passengers, had pieced together a theory.

There was a bad part on the plane. There wasn't a replacement part at the airport, so the airline was flying one in. When the part landed, maintenance crews would need an hour to install it. Most of the time would be dismantling half the jet to get to the bad part. The actual installation of the new part was said to be easy.

Our passenger network buzzed with each new bit of data. "The part is on its way." "I heard the pilots are coming back to the plane." "US Air has a Miami connection through Pittsburgh leaving at one o'clock."

Our small group had shrunk since 6:00 a.m. Some folks found alternatives. Others rebooked for the following day.

A flight attendant in the know had told us that our plane was needed in Miami, so the flight would not be cancelled.

Hostages bond with, even come to love their captors. It's called the Stockholm syndrome. I think it's called that because you have time to fly to Stockholm and back before your flight leaves. So we waited. By two o'clock, there were only seven of us left, including my new bride and me.

An hour later the most amazing thing happened: we boarded the plane. Our connection had left Miami at 12:30 p.m., some two and a half hours earlier, but we could catch an Air Jamaica flight at 5:20 p.m. If we got off the ground quickly, we might make it.

An empty airplane turns coach into first class. Four flight attendants were there to serve the seven of us. Our joy was short-lived.

The plane taxied to the end of the runway. The captain pulled back on the throttle. We started to roll and *KA-BOOM*, something exploded. My eyes got big and my sphincter got small. I grabbed my new wife's hand. The takeoff was aborted, and the plane diverted off the runway.

If there's one thing that undermines your confidence in a recently repaired aircraft, it's a freaking explosion. I was happy to be returning to our friendly little terminal. But instead of taking us home, the pilot turned the plane around and headed back to the runway.

"Sorry about that," the intercom crackled. "What you heard was a backfire. Sometimes in a crosswind like we have this afternoon, the top engine doesn't get enough air in the intake to get going. That's what happened. So we're going try it again. It should be fine." Or something like that—I was still hyperventilating.

Once again he fired up the engines, and after a seven-and-a-half-hour delay, we were on our way to Jamaica.

At this point, it is fair to ask what any of this has to do with advertising. That experience is comparable to a day in the ad business. You plan the best you can. Frequent and frustrating delays crop up. You have hope, then experience disappointment, then hope again. Just when you think you've overcome every obstacle, an explosion sends you back to the starting gate.

Advertising is a business for relentless personalities. You must be both goal-oriented and extremely flexible. A very large part of getting the job done is just hanging in there. So when you do finally succeed, it can feel almost as good as going on your honeymoon. Almost.

Resetting to zero

ONE FINE DAY, I destroyed a small neighborhood. It was an abandoned neighborhood on a closed military base near Sacramento, California.

We were shooting a commercial about the Army National Guard's disaster relief capabilities. Most communities will not allow you to demolish them to shoot a commercial. We were fortunate to find this ghost town.

Before we could smash the place up, we had to cut the lawns and touch up the homes, to give it a lived-in look. So when we destroyed it, it appeared as a normal neighborhood that was hit by a hurricane.

This all proceeded pretty much on schedule. The client, Colonel Mauro Cooper, and I agreed on most of the military equipment, the choppers, Humvees and trucks. But we disagreed on the ambulances. Coop wanted to use ambulances with large red crosses on the side. I didn't.

My position was that the red crosses made the ambulances look like they were from the Red Cross. This would take the focus off the Army National Guard and potentially confuse people. Hey, the Red Cross is a great organization. But they can do their own commercials. After a lengthy discussion, I convinced him to see the error of his ways and he came around to my position. There would be no red crosses on the ambulances.

When the ambulances showed up for filming, there were red crosses on the side! He had changed back to his original position. He had reset to zero.

Resetting to zero is a common advertising phenomenon. Let me explain. My mother had an old baking timer that she set by turning a handle to the number of minutes she wanted something to cook. A soft tic-tic-ticking meant the timer was on. As the minutes melted away the timer would reset to zero. Buzzing when it was back where it started.

In the ad business, this occurs when a client must be moved to a new point of view. Over the course of a meeting, the agency makes a case for its position. With luck, the client listens and responds favorably to the agency's thinking.

The agency goes away believing that the client now accepts their perspective. At the next meeting, however, the client has reverted to his old position as if the previous meeting had never taken place. In the agency's absence, he resets to zero minus the buzzing.

The process is as predictable as burnt toast. Most clients do it. If you listen closely you can almost hear them tic-tic-ticking.

There's an old expression in sales. Once you sell the suit, you can stop selling the buttons. With many clients, however, to keep them from resetting to zero, you have to keep selling the buttons.

On the set in Sacramento, we shot the ambulances with red crosses visible. Then, in the editing suite, I tried to minimize their screen time and feature the Guard soldiers so it wouldn't come off as a Red Cross commercial. It worked fine.

In the end, we created a realistic disaster without enduring one ourselves.

Do you need a Hispanic advertising agency?

VIRTUALLY EVERYONE IN MARKETING knows the story of the Chevy Nova. The Nova was said to have sold poorly in Spanish-speaking countries because the name Nova, or "no va," translates into "doesn't go."

It's a great story. It's not true, but it's a great story. Its legacy is as a cautionary tale when dealing with Spanish-speaking markets. And if current demographic trends hold, we will all be dealing with Spanish-speaking markets.

So should you hire a Hispanic advertising agency? Ask a Hispanic advertising agency that question and the answer will always be "*sì*."

I've had to answer this question for various clients, and, depending on the circumstances, I've come up with different answers. The recommendation is dependent on a couple of factors. First, how large is the Hispanic market for your product? Is it large enough to generate the revenue to cover the cost of a second agency?

You can be certain your new agency will advise you of the need for a new campaign. They will cite a thousand different reasons the existing campaign is wrong. Chief among these reasons is that the new agency didn't create it. They won't say that, but no agency wants to extend someone else's effort. It makes us feel dirty.

If you recall the pseudo Menudo commercial I mentioned earlier, that work was not done by a Hispanic agency. We used the Puerto Rico office of our shop. They retained the look and feel of our American spot. It is highly unlikely an outside agency would have created such a strong companion.

One thing that will always bite you when working on the Hispanic market is the Spanish language. Most of us tend to think of Spanish as a single dialect. It's not. In the United States there are, at least, four different common dialects. In the northeast, Spanish is spoken with Puerto Rican flavor. The Middle Atlantic States have a Central American accent because of the large El Salvadoran population. In Miami, there is a heavy Cuban influence. In Texas, Tex-Mex is king, and the Tex-Mex of the Lone Star State differs from the Spanish spoken in the Mexican neighborhoods of East Los Angeles.

If you are producing a national radio spot, pick your poison. Don't worry, you'll be wrong. You cannot make the right choice, because the right choice doesn't exist. I have been told that there is Castilian Spanish that is fairly neutral and passes for a universal Spanish. I've had radio spots translated into this "neutral" Spanish. The response is universal. It is universally disliked.

Mercifully, there are now two large networks, Telemundo and Univision, that provide a reference for national Spanish translation. However, when you have the chance to tailor your spots geographically, that is a better route to travel.

My view is that a company is better off having Hispanic writers and art directors who are part of the mainstream of your agency. We live in a multicultural society. Their perspectives are valuable on any number of accounts, inside and outside of the Hispanic community.

Extending the idea of a separate agency for Hispanics to its logical extreme leads to endless segmentation of your account. Should you hire an African American agency to reach your African American audience? How about women? Should you hire an agency that specializes in female advertising? And why stop at audiences? You can hire a direct mail marketing firm to handle the direct mail portion of your business. Naturally, an internet marketing firm for banner ads and key word search would also make sense. Don't forget to get a social network marketing shop as well.

Except that none of that makes sense. That's why you hired a full-service advertising agency in the first place. So that your company would look, feel and speak like it's coming from one place.

That way, when you talk to any segment, including the Hispanic segment, you are including them in, rather than separating them out.

Mr. Humble

DURING NEW BUSINESS PITCHES I've run across a number of interesting characters, none more bizarre than the owner of a software company in Arlington, Virginia.

New business pitches are often chemistry checks, a chance to sit down and figure out if you like each other and if you would be comfortable working together. Sometimes you hit it off, sometimes you don't.

One particular pitch started normally. Our team presented agency credentials, listened to the needs and wants of the company, asked and answered questions. It was all very cordial and nice.

About a half-hour into the session, the president of the firm, who had planted himself firmly at the head of the table, began to speak. He talked about the company philosophy and then launched into a long-winded description of himself and how he had built the company.

The thing he most desired in employees and business partners was humility. His company was built on humility. He made sure that everyone associated with his company was humble.

Then, he looked us in he eye and told us that no one was more humble than he.

"I can prove that I am the most humble person at this company," he said. "I have told everyone here that anyone more humble than me can have my job, they can be the president. And it hasn't happened yet. Because no one is more humble than me."

He finished with a flourish and sat there wearing an extremely self-satisfied smile. We were quiet. Stunned, actually.

Bragging to prove your humility is like fornicating to prove your virginity.

At that point, I knew we didn't want to work with this crazy little man. But ad agencies are terrific at rationalization. Perhaps, once the working relationship began, he wouldn't be part of the picture. The potential clients in the room were pretty nice. They had probably heard this strange speech before, and it hadn't seemed to harm them in any way.

We played out the rest of the meeting. We demonstrated our humbleness by remarking over and over how important it was to be humble. We thanked the president for his humbleness. We extolled his humbleness. We were humbled by his humbleness. We ended the meeting bowing and scraping and luxuriating in humility. We humbly exited.

About a week later, we received a phone call from the marketing director. They had chosen another advertising agency. We were humbled.

Segmenting your audience

AGENCIES SPEND MILLIONS AND millions of bucks segmenting demographics. They slice the market thick and thin. Niches and subgroups are uncovered and explored.

But at the end of the day, every single client can divide his prospects exactly the same way. It doesn't matter if you're selling cars or carrots. Here are your five basic targets.

1) Got 'em. These are your current customers. They know you. They like what you're selling. You can increase profits by getting them to buy your stuff more often, or to buy your stuff in greater quantities, or to buy a higher quality of your stuff and, if they are not already, to buy product line extensions. They are the simplest group for you to reach because you already got 'em. Get it?

2) Should get 'em. These are the folks who use or need a product like yours. They are similar in makeup to your

current customers. They may not be aware of your product or may be buying from a competitor. Simple awareness advertising or some type of trial promotion is all that's required.

3) Could get 'em. These prospects are only worth pursuing if they are a good value. Ask yourself, are they cheap to target? Are they likely to respond to your message? If the answer is yes, then spending a small portion of your budget on these folks is warranted.

4) Might get 'em. You will not convert these prospects in large numbers. They are well outside your core demographic. There may be a special occasion or reason to talk to these folks. You might also consider them when looking at your media waste. Chasing these consumers will get the brand manager fired.

5) Forget 'em. Yep, it's true. Consumers exist who will not buy your product. Woo them at your peril. They don't need you. They don't want you. Some of 'em might actually hate you. Ignore them.

As easy as this system is to understand, it is hard to follow. It is many a client's natural inclination to pursue every possible customer. As an adman, it's my responsibility to knock that crazy notion right out of your head.

Identify these segments for your product any way you like, demographically, psychographically or just by using plain ole English. Try it. It works. You will discover your most fertile target. Because, amazingly, every product or service has exactly the same segments.

Got 'em. Should get 'em. Could get 'em. Might get 'em. Forget 'em.

Now go get 'em.

Bullets

COPYWRITERS HATE BULLETS. MOST would rather have a bullet put into their brain than have one put into their copy.

Bullets in advertising are the small dots that precede a word or phrase in an ad. They are used to indicate importance. They look like this:

- Cheesy

- Lame

- Useless

The reason they are called bullets is they look like the hole that would be left behind if a bullet went through the page. Bullets don't always have to look like bullet holes to be called bullets. They can be little diamonds, stars, pointing fingers, almost anything.

Bullets are part of a group of attention-getting graphic devices that have their origin in retailing. There are bullets, bursts and snipes.

If copywriters hate bullets, art directors absolutely convulse in revulsion over bursts and snipes. The burst is a patch of color that sits on top of an ad, usually with a jagged outline. It is also called a sunburst or starburst because its color is often yellow or orange. Words like *NEW* or *IMPROVED* are positioned in the burst or breaking out of it. Sometimes both *NEW* and *IMPROVED* are in the same burst. The burst is guaranteed to ruin any layout, because it tells you that the rest of the ad is unimportant.

Snipes are banners that run diagonally over and across the corner of an ad. *NEW* and *IMPROVED* are also commonly found in snipes. *FOR A LIMITED TIME* is also popular. Once again, the snipe screams that the words inside the snipe are the ones that deserve your attention. The rest of the ad, not so much.

I can reluctantly admit that bullets, bursts and snipes do have a place. That place is on a package. Since a package always looks the same, these devices call attention to themselves by changing the appearance of a package.

The words *NEW* and *IMPROVED* can achieve the same result. It may get a customer to take a second look at a product they have previously passed by.

Since bullets, bursts and snipes worked on packages, some brand manager figured they would probably work on ads as well. It's roughly equivalent to the concept that udders work on a cow, so let's put them on a bull.

Rather than adding anything, they detract from the rest of the ad. When done properly, an ad is crafted to lead a reader to take a certain action. Splashing a burst or snipe across it makes that impossible.

I suppose if you ran the same ad all the time, a burst would make some readers notice it. But you shouldn't be running the same ad constantly in the first place. Your ads should be varied, changing and evolving.

Ad copy should be engaging, enticing, romancing. It should be SELLING. None of those things are possible with bullets. They are a distraction, diverting attention to only themselves.

As I said, bursts, snipes and bullets have a place. But when you use them incorrectly, you're aiming the gun at yourself.

External forces

THE VIRGINIA RAILWAY EXPRESS, the VRE, is the Washington, DC, equivalent of the Long Island Railroad. It's a heavy rail commuter line that connects downtown with the burbs.

When LMO won VRE, we prepared a multimedia campaign with television, radio and print elements. Everything kicked off the same day. At that time, normal VRE daily ridership count was about four thousand passengers. The day we launched the campaign, ridership dropped to under two thousand.

It was a disaster. Literally. There had been a derailment. The VRE shared right of way with CSX. One of their freight trains had ripped up the tracks; hence VRE could run only a very limited schedule, resulting in a huge drop in passenger counts. Circumstances beyond our control had negated the effects of our campaign.

Fortunately, the fine folks at the Virginia Railway Express didn't hold the agency accountable for the poor results of the product launch. But they could have. The agency is often a convenient place to park blame.

The CSX derailment is a dramatic example of advertising's place in marketing and sales. As important as it is to your overall success, it cannot drive success against larger forces. If your product sucks, no amount of advertising will make it fly off the shelves. Ironically, good advertising will kill a bad product faster than no advertising. Good advertising will induce consumers to try your product. Trial will produce a bad reaction and bad word of mouth. Soon everyone will know your product stinks. Sales will drop off a cliff. In such a case, no advertising might allow a bad product to limp along much longer. If your product is a dog, this is the best you can hope for. Eventually, though, bad products disappear with or without advertising.

The most well known example of a product collapse as a result of external circumstances is the Tylenol scare of 1982. That autumn, a psychopath in Chicago took bottles of Tylenol Extra Strength off of store shelves, laced individual capsules with lethal doses of cyanide, then returned the bottles to the shelves. In short order, seven people were dead. The deaths made national news, and sales of Tylenol dropped to nothing.

The reaction of Johnson & Johnson is now a textbook case of successful crisis management. They alerted retailers and the medical community. They withdrew the product from stores. The company even offered Tylenol tablets to customers who returned their Tylenol capsules to the company. Finally, they couponed like crazy.

Rather than cover their butts, they were forthright and honest. Johnson & Johnson put the safety of the public ahead of their profits. It was an expensive choice. It cost hundreds of millions of dollars. But at the end of the day, it saved the brand.

Years ago, Schlitz was the best selling beer in America. It was "The Beer That Made Milwaukee Famous." It had "gusto."

The executives at Schlitz decided if they could brew the beer faster, they could produce and sell more beer. They embraced a process using high temperature fermentation, allowing Schlitz to be speed brewed. The following year they set records for the amount of beer they sold. A year after that, sales began to drop.

Speed brewing produced more beer. It also produced a less desirable product. The brand was severely damaged.

Imagine if Schlitz had used a crisis management approach. If they went public and told the world they had changed their brewing process and ruined their beer. That they had made a mistake and wanted their customers back. And to get them back, Schlitz would discount like crazy.

Would it have worked? We'll never know. We do know that the former No. 1 selling beer in America is now a minor brand. We know that ignoring the problem didn't work.

In the VRE's case, there was no need to get the story out. The derailment was big news. Still, press releases were sent out immediately apologizing for the inconvenience and detailing the steps the VRE was taking to work around the derailment. New schedules were drawn up, printed and distributed. A substantial new-rider program including free tickets was instituted before the disruption was extended.

It took a while for the VRE to get back on track. But the honest and proactive approach paid dividends. Over time, service and confidence were restored. Eventually, ridership almost quadrupled to fifteen thousand a day.

The explosion in passengers led to a new problem. Trains were full. Parking lots were full. The need to attract new riders was over. Our agency was fired and replaced by a lobbying firm that could help the VRE get more state money for expansion. Success had created its own external force, and we had become an external agency!

Stupid human tricks

WE WERE IN THE hallway playing stupid human tricks, when a young account executive said an amazing thing. "I can touch my forehead to my ankles." Before the gasps of disbelief had subsided, Sean folded like a wallet, touched her forehead to her ankles and snapped back up. "Can't everyone?"

Well, no.

That demonstration drove home a lesson. We undervalue our own gifts. Anything we find easy, we assume others find easy as well. Can't everyone?

Recognizing your gifts is critical to a successful career. I know mine. I remember what clients say during meetings. This allows me to create ads for the next meeting that the client loves. It's a good gift.

Finding your gift can be difficult. I was oblivious to mine. A coworker's comment made me aware. While we walked out of a meeting, he said, "Nice job, Mr. Elephant." I had no idea what this meant and returned silence. He continued, "You remember everything."

It hit me. What he was saying was that I had a better memory than he did. That I had the best memory in the room. I was an elephant, and an elephant never forgets. I had discovered my edge, my advantage, my gift.

There are all kinds of gifts. A few are obvious. If you can draw, you have probably known it since grade school. If you always finished at the top of your class, you have enough smarts to know your advantage. A handsome or pretty face is a common gift. If you have one, you know it. If you don't, you know it too. The answer greets you in the mirror every morning.

People are attracted to attractive people. Duh. Take a look at the CEOs of the Fortune 500 companies, and you'll find a lot of nice-looking folks. There are exceptions, but for the most part CEOs look like they come from central casting. You will doubtlessly find competent managers behind most of those perfectly lined teeth, but make no mistake, that perfect gray coiffure accounts for a part of their success.

A deep, rich speaking voice is a wonderful gift. If you sound like James Earl Jones, people will listen when you speak, even if you have nothing to say.

One account executive I know took a beating every week from a very difficult client who would chew him up and spit him out over any little thing. But he was always back at the job smiling the next day. Like Wolverine from the X-Men, he healed immediately after being wounded.

An underappreciated gift is the ability to sleep on airplanes. Some folks can do it. Others can't. I'm in the latter category. I have often watched with envy as coworkers nodded off on our way to an out-of-town meeting, arriving rested and refreshed at our destination.

Speaking of rare abilities, very few possess the self-control to keep their mouth shut. Knowing when to say nothing is a remarkable talent.

Finding your gift is a voyage of self-discovery. You might be gregarious, likable, detail-oriented, relentless, tough-skinned, quick-witted or disciplined. Almost everyone has some physical or personality trait that gives them an advantage. If you're lucky, you already know it. If not, keep looking. And if you try, who knows, you may be able to bend over and touch your head to your ankles.

Leaping to conclusions

WHEN I INFORMED MY father that I had joined a gym, he gave me some advice. "Don't get muscle-bound."

Dad had given me loads of strange advice over the years, but this piece of wisdom ranked right up there. At the time, I weighed 145 pounds. My chance of developing any definition was unlikely. To become muscle-bound would take an act of God.

A lifetime of dealing with my father had taught me not to react to his outrageous comments. First, I took take a deep breath and agreed with him. "Well, Dad, that can be a problem." Then I walked back from the edge. "A lot of my time will be doing cardio, not lifting." Finally, I changed the conversation. "And this gym is rated one of the best in the city."

I am not muscle-bound, nor am I in danger of said boundness. Joining a health club was a good idea. And it has kept me pretty fit over the years. I'm not a gym rat. I work out to be able to eat and drink what I like without growing into a special on The Learning Channel.

Nevertheless, those sage words from my old man have proven useful. Not in the matter of my physique, though. Rather, many clients share the same tendency to leap to the extremes.

When I was working on Flav-O-Rich cottage cheese, a large Southeastern brand, I suggested that a coupon on the package might impact sales. Our client didn't hesitate to leap to the extreme. "I don't want to be the kind of company that gives its product away."

In his mind, a single coupon, for a few cents off, for a limited time, had magically morphed into the transformational event in the history of the company, changing the image of the entire organization. I took a deep breath. Agreed with the client. "I don't want folks to think you're that kind of company either." Walked back from the edge. "But I do want to be the kind of company that believes so strongly in our products that we are willing to let potential customers sample our product inexpensively." Changed the conversation. "Because I believe if we induce trial, this product will convert samplers to regular purchasers."

On another occasion, I was in a position to help a charity golf tournament get an NBA player to lend his name to their event. This would have helped to get the word out and lend some star power to the fundraiser. When I voiced this possibility, the director of the charity looked at me and said, "We don't want to be a celebrity-driven organization."

Mind you, this charity hadn't used a celebrity of any type for years. They had as much chance of becoming celebrity-driven as some skinny kid had of becoming muscle-bound.

I could come up with dozens of examples. But the solution is always the same. Take a deep breath, agree, walk back from the edge and change the conversation. It doesn't always work. We never hooked up with the celeb. But this is a reasonable technique for dealing with folks who leap to hasty conclusions.

Sometimes when people add one and one they come up with ten thousand for an answer. To be perfectly honest, we all do it. The key to responding to these types of reactions is treating them as if they make sense. So, instead of responding with your true feelings or becoming defensive, take that breath. Sometimes, that's all that is necessary to keep a meeting moving forward.

I have avoided countless arguments by using this technique. And that is the real point. Once you get into a disagreement with a client, you've lost. It doesn't matter if you're right or wrong. When you and the client are on opposite sides, you lose. In the immortal words of Patrick Swayze, "Nobody wins a fight."

Inevitably, there will be times when there are differences of opinion. Discussed in the proper fashion, it's healthy. But from my desk, the job of an advertising agency is to recommend. To give advice. To give good counsel. To lead a horse to water. None of that is possible from an adversarial position.

Then again, if I joined a gym and got muscle-bound, I could beat up my clients and force them to submit to my ideas.

It's a tempting thought but one that would ultimately prove self-defeating. It's much better to take a deep breath, step back from the edge and change the conversation.

Meetingsmanship

THAT ISN'T REALLY A word. It should be. Meetings consume a meaningful portion of our lives. Yet often, the only preparation for a meeting is figuring out the list of attendees. That is unfair to everyone on the list.

Meetingsmanship means understanding that meetings are about control. Exercising that control starts with clearly identifying a preferred outcome before sending out a memo or meeting maker. Without a defined objective, your meeting will go on endlessly and reach an unsatisfactory conclusion. A ship without a destination can never reach port.

Like a ship, a meeting can be hijacked. The agenda can be changed midstream, or a side issue can move front and center. It's easy to end up with a massive, unproductive exercise in useless.

I've been in advertising for thirty-two years. Conservatively, I've spent five hours a week in meetings. That's five hours a week, fifty weeks a year (allowing for vacation), for thirty-two years. Do the math. I've spent eight thousand hours, or nearly a year of my life, in meetings. If that's not horrifying enough, consider that half that time was wasted. That's six months of wasted.

I have always been fascinated by how much time I spend on airplanes, on the toilet, whatever. Take elevators. I ride lifts about five minutes a day. Multiply that times five days a week, times fifty weeks a year, times thirty years, that comes out to 37,500 minutes. Divide that by sixty minutes, divide that by twenty-four hours, and I've spent over twenty-six days in elevators.

It's a minor compulsion. I have it reasonably under control. I once calculated that over the years, I've consumed 110 pounds of powdered non-dairy coffee creamer. That's a Kate Beckinsale of non-dairy creamer. I wish.

I once saw the following lines of prose on a colleague's office door:

Are you lonely?
Don't like working on your own?
Hate making decisions?
Call a meeting.
You can see people, draw flow charts, feel important, form subcommittees, impress your colleagues, make meaningless recommendations, all on company time.
Meetings, the practical alternative to work.

The commentary above describes an advertising archetype. There are more than a few such people in your office. Make sure you know who they are.

The real issue is how to put the time you spend in meetings to good use. First, as I said, meetings are about control. Even if it isn't your meeting, you can provide guidance for everyone in the room by asking the right questions. It's easy to do. I play dumb, which I am incredibly good at. I start with the most basic question, "Whose meeting is this?" I immediately follow up with a question for them. "What are we trying to accomplish in this meeting?" You'll be amazed at how well this defines the parameters of the discussion.

When you are the one convening your coworkers, define your objective, send an agenda, set a time limit, give them appropriate materials ahead of time. Think control.

Preparation breeds confidence. Know what you are going to say. Practice. Lead the group to the conclusion you desire. Sun Tzu, in *The Art of War*, says every battle is won before it is fought. He is talking about your meeting.

Once you have achieved your desired outcome, end the meeting. You are done. Finished. Do not continue, or everything you have accomplished can unravel.

I once gave a creative presentation that came to a satisfactory conclusion. The client had approved a television spot for production. On the way out the door, our respected and beloved account guy said off-handedly to the client, "Do you want us to revise any of the other spots?" This allowed the client to second-guess himself, and he decided he would like all the spots revised so he could look at them again.

A casual comment had undone the entire meeting and the days of work that had preceded it. We did not kill the account executive. He was our friend. But in the words of the Queen, we were not amused.

Try this. Think of a meeting like you would think of a date. You know where and when it's going to start. You plan a series of events that leads toward a positive conclusion. If something unexpected happens, you make the best of it and try to steer back on course. When you reach your goal, you do not ask your date to reconsider.

If you really want to be successful, prepare for a meeting like you would for a date with Kate Beckinsale.

Mulligans

IN GOLF THERE'S A THING called a mulligan. It's when you hit your shot so badly you simply drop another ball and try again. A synonym is a "do-over."

Advertising is the mulligan capital of the world. There is hardly any part of the process that doesn't get at least a minor do-over. Part of that has to do with collaboration. When many hands touch a project, many changes follow.

Unrealistic deadlines also lead to mulligans. Rushing through any process results in inadequate quality control. The outcome is usually unsatisfactory. Hence, the do-over.

A Budweiser television producer once lamented to me, "There's never time to do it right, but there is always time to do it over." That's worth repeating. There's never time to do it right, but there is always time to do it over.

Which brings me to a touchstone that applies not only to advertising but to every business or project that has been attempted in human history. It's a triangle. On each side is a word. The three words are cheap, good and fast. In the center of the triangle is a phrase. You can have any two.

Pick two: cheap and good, fine. To accomplish that will take a while, so you won't be able to have it fast. You want it fast and good? Be prepared to pay overtime and rush charges, and don't expect discounts. Cheap and fast? Can do, but don't expect the *Mona Lisa*.

When you want cheap, fast and good? Prepare to be disappointed. You cannot have all three. You will end up with cheap and fast.

Good takes time. Good takes money. In fact, if you want more than good, if you want excellent, slow and expensive gives you the best chance. Never forget Schlitz—good was sacrificed at the altar of cheap and fast. The brand never recovered; they never got a mulligan.

A mulligan is a good thing. There are times when there is no substitute for a do-over. One of the foibles of the human condition is imperfection. Recognizing and correcting mistakes is a sign of intelligence.

You can avoid most mistakes by giving yourself time to do it right. But if you have to have it now, prepare to make time to do it over.

Unfocused groups

FOCUS GROUPS ARE MUCH maligned and rightly so. Creatives hate them. The information they produce tends to be obvious. Yet, focus groups are the most common way that agencies probe the opinions of consumers.

The venue is highly artificial, a room with no windows and a large mirror on one wall. Ten or twelve people sit around a table and are led through a discussion about a product or service by a moderator. Even the best moderators have to pinch themselves to stay awake during these mind-numbing sessions.

The only reason folks show up is that they are paid for their opinions. They are the best folks that a hundred bucks can buy. These opinions are then written down and thrown away.

Almost every group has some guy who thinks he has a preferred view of reality and tries to hijack the conversation. He wastes everyone's time with his important insights on chewing gum, which is fine, because everyone's time is being wasted anyway.

The group will also feature a couple of participants who sit quietly without uttering a word until the moderator asks them to speak. When they finally do, you wish they had remained quiet.

Every now and again, you run across someone who thinks they are being filmed for a hidden camera commercial. In an attempt to collect the millions of dollars they believe they will be paid if chosen, they gush endlessly about the product as if it were the savior of mankind. This delights clients immensely.

The agency sits behind a two-way mirror so we can monitor every syllable. After the process drags on for a couple of hours, just as the agency is about to drink hemlock, the session ends. Alas, eight or twelve more people walk in for the second two-hour session.

The good news is that the research facility usually provides food and candy for the people behind the mirror. I can get a decent sugar buzz if I gobble enough Raisinets and M&Ms.

Eventually, a focus group will turn negative. Caustic comments are usually funny, and once a couple come out, group members try to outdo each other. Once the piling on begins in earnest, it gets nasty. This is my favorite part of the night. This is where the campaign that the client forced on you meets its demise.

As this small group gleefully shreds every headline and visual, the client has nowhere to go. This is the only socially redeeming value of a focus group. Those consumers on the other side of the glass will say things you could NEVER say to your client. Things he doesn't want to hear from anyone.

Even in the best client/agency relationships, there are areas where the client won't take your word. An independent source is needed to make your point, to give you credibility. Watching a focus group turn into a bunch of baboons at a safari park ripping the vinyl roof off the top of a Camaro can strongly make your point. You don't have to say a word.

Almost makes one think that focus groups are worthwhile. Almost.

Immediacy

IN THE CIVIL WAR, there was a Southern general named Nathan Bedford Forrest. Though not as well known as Robert E. Lee or Ulysses S. Grant, he is considered by many to have been the finest commander of his time. A brilliant yet largely uneducated man, he has been mostly forgotten by history, and, given his postwar life, that is probably for the best.

Forrest's strategy in battle was simple: "Get there firstest with the mostest." This ungrammatical phrase, uttered by an ignorant, racist man, is one that marketers ignore at their own peril. Get to your consumers first with the strongest possible message.

This has never been truer than it is today. There has been a seismic change in the advertising business in the past few years, and it can be boiled down to one word: *immediacy*.

The speed at which an idea, once conceived, can be communicated has shrunk to a few hours. On some accounts we change our strategy and our executions daily. This is possible only because new media operates in real time.

It can take eight weeks to produce a television commercial. An internet banner can be created in hours and be in front of a consumer within minutes. By clicking, a consumer can respond to the banner in seconds. The time between contact with that consumer and his response takes place in the now. It is immediate.

Things that weren't considered media five years ago are now part of our arsenal. Smartphones make you part of your customer's hand. You are literally in physical contact.

The really good news is that we can process information and respond almost as fast as the information is brought into existence. When you visit a website, we can collect your information, create a contextual profile and have an email in your inbox before you leave the site.

In essence, an advertiser can take the competition out of the equation. You can make a sale before the customer is even aware you have competition. But you have to get there first with a compelling offer. Firstest with the mostest.

If you have an established brand, even better. New tools like texting, hashtags and QR codes are a great way to leverage your existing strength. Like the comic said, "It took me years to become an overnight success."

There is synergy between old and new media. One doesn't destroy the other. They multiply each other. A magazine ad is a great place to ask consumers to contact you. The ad should also carry a branding message that enhances the value of the brand, thereby improving the response rate.

A tool we often use at LMO is to create a unique landing page for a certain ad or campaign. That way we know that every visitor to the page was motivated by that piece. It's a great way to track effectiveness. It also shows clients what they are getting for their money.

As technology races forward, new opportunities will present themselves. The interval between products and consumers will continue to shrink. Wise marketers will pay heed to the words of a dead Confederate general.

The United States Holocaust Memorial Museum

CREATING THE ADVERTISING FOR the opening of the United States Holocaust Memorial Museum presented some unique challenges. For starters, I'm an Italian Catholic.

Second, most folks visit Washington to see the cherry blossoms or visit the Smithsonian. We wanted to compel people to visit a place where the very worst of humanity is on display. Although a significant part of the museum is dedicated to the bravery, courage and indomitable spirit of those who faced genocide, the facts of the Holocaust would be displayed in a brutally honest fashion.

There was a third complication. The museum was the culmination of years of planning and dreaming. But not everyone shared the same dream. In fact, there were three separate and strong-willed groups of clients.

We were hired by the museum staff, the folks who found the exhibits and put the museum together. They would manage and maintain the USHMM. Their vision of the museum was built around attracting the largest, most diverse group of visitors possible.

Another group who had a different vision of the museum were the Holocaust survivors. To them the museum was personal. They had very strong opinions on how the museum should tell their story. Their opinions didn't always mesh with those of the museum staff. Obviously, their views would have a major impact on how our advertising was presented to the public.

The third and no less important group were the large donors. Without them, there would be no Memorial Museum. And when you pony up a few million dollars, you expect your opinion to matter.

Balancing these sometimes intense differences was a challenge. Making the task even more difficult was the fact that there was less than uniformity of opinion inside the groups as well.

As an ad guy in the middle of a situation like this, you do two things. First, you duck. You don't take sides. You keep your opinions to yourself about everything except the very narrow concerns that pertain exclusively to marketing. Second, when asked your opinion, you begin every answer with the phrase, "From an advertising perspective . . ."

When the group comes to consensus, you act.

Although working on an account like the Memorial Museum is a serious task, it turned out to be fun. Even with the disagreements, there was a sense of unity and purpose. And watching the museum grow was exciting.

We would tour the museum in hardhats every month as it was being built. These visits continued, sans hats, as the exhibits were being installed. In the midst of this memorial to unimaginable horror, one incident always made me smile. The folks putting the collection together found a railway car in Poland. It was the exact style and model of the boxcars that were used by the Nazis to shuttle prisoners to the concentration camps. It was old and weather-beaten and looked authentic and scary.

The Polish government agreed to ship the car to the museum free of charge. Then they went one better. They cleaned, refurbished and painted the car, so, when it arrived, it looked brand new.

Gone was the foreboding image it had portrayed in its previous state. The museum was forced to spend money to have an artist weather and disrepair the car back to its former state. *Oy vey*. You'll see that weathered boxcar if you visit the museum.

Eventually, it became time to create the ads for the opening. After a number of rounds, we settled on a simple and powerful idea. We used actual newspaper headlines that proclaimed, "Whispers of genocide growing," and, "Secret files detail torture mass killings." The headlines slowly turned black from heat, then caught fire. We shot at high speed so the burn-through and curling ashes moved almost gracefully.

The copy talked about the museum opening and its meaning. It ended with a sentence that let the viewers know the headlines in the spot were not from World War II. They were contemporary.

The voice-over was delivered with chilling impact by Stockard Channing. You may not be aware of this, but Stockard has one of the most sought-after voices for commercials. She's amazing; she can do anything. Her voice is an instrument.

We didn't meet in person. The session was conducted over the phone. Stockard was in a studio in, I think, California, and I was across the country in New York. It is the best performance of any voice-over talent I've ever used.

The ads were very well received. The opening was a major event. Over the years, the United States Holocaust Memorial Museum has become an important institution. Its message is timeless. It will certainly outlast me. It's also very satisfying to know I played a small part in its success.

My personal discovery was that even working with the most horrifying material could be uplifting. Creating the advertising for the opening was a wonderful experience shared with dedicated and talented folks. And, though we were surrounded by reminders of a terrible tragedy, there was much to find a smile about.

Stress

A YOUNG ACCOUNT EXECUTIVE once told me, "Anything in life can be made better by buying a new sweater." In her case, there was no doubt it was true. Barbara Christen had a bounce in her step when she walked the halls in a recently purchased cashmere cardigan.

Attitude counts for a lot. In a business that demands resiliency, knowing how to alter your attitude is a must. Barb was miles ahead of the rest of us.

Most well-adjusted adult humans have come to terms with the fact that you cannot control what happens to you. There will be surprises, disappointments and disasters in your life.

What you can control is how you react to these circumstances. That, however, is easier said than done. Buying a new sweater doesn't work for everyone. There is an entire industry dedicated to relieving stress and teaching you how to make lemonade from lemons.

Walk into a bookstore and take a gander at the size of the self-help section. Self-help books, there's perversion of the language. It's a help book. It's not a self-help book unless you wrote the book to help yourself. If it's written by Dr. Phil, it's only self-help if it's written for Dr. Phil.

When things go south at LMO, I usually look around the room and say, "We chose this profession." It is my way of reminding folks that we are where we want to be. That we have pretty good jobs. That a lot of folks would like to be in our place, and that we have to take the bad with the good.

I also have my own little stress-reducing exercise I perform when I feel pressure. I sit in a chair, hang my arms at my sides, relax my shoulders and forearms, spread my fingers and mentally picture St. Elmo's fire escaping my fingertips and being absorbed into the ground.

I don't know why it works. I don't care why it works. It just does. Yep, it's a little odd, but as I imagine the electrical discharges leaving my body, so does the stress.

Try it. It's cheaper than buying a new sweater.

Render walkabout

Industrial Light and Magic (ILM) is the company that George Lucas created to produce special effects for his Star Wars movies. It remains one of the finest special effects shops on the planet and is in constant use producing effects for movies. For a while they had a commercial production side.

Much of ILM is devoted to computer graphics. Rendering the high quality of visual effects you see on a motion picture screen takes a tremendous amount of computer power. I've walked though the render farm at ILM. It is the size of a convenience store and filled with row upon row of very large computers. The processing power is so great that when it's not being used to render special effects, it is sometimes leased to the United States Navy to run simulations of ocean waves.

The fellow walking me around ILM told me that the electronics are so powerful that, on one occasion, the configuration of the room had to be rearranged; otherwise they would produced enough microwaves to be harmful to humans.

Even the simplest effects take time to render. Just like on your home computer, an estimate of the time the computer needs to create the effect comes up on the screen. At ILM, on some of the larger pieces, it may take twenty or forty minutes before you can look at your scene.

Which means you have nothing to do for twenty or forty minutes. Rather than wait in a darkened edit bay, the editors at ILM have a practice known as render walkabout.

Walking around the facility you bump into other groups doing the same. You learn who is in town, what other editors are working on, what problems they've encountered and you get the opportunity to trade information. I have to say that this is one of the more pleasant workplace diversions I have stumbled across.

In the middle of the group of nondescript buildings that make up ILM is a coffee trailer, called Java the Hut, surrounded by a few small tables and some metal chairs. Plastic alien plants and trees left over from the Tim Burton remake of *Planet of the Apes* are scattered around. Many of the walkabouts end up here. The coffee is decent.

When your time is up, you head back to the editing bay to see what magic the computer has spawned. Sometimes it is great, sometimes it needs to be tweaked or changed. If so, the new instructions are loaded into the computer and, once again, it is time for a render walkabout.

In the years since my last visit to ILM, the company has moved across the Golden Gate Bridge to a new facility in the Presidio. I sincerely hope that render walkabout made the journey with them.

The mission is based on good nutrition

IT'S A SAFE GUESS that two of the most beloved words in advertising are "craft services." For the unfamiliar, craft services refers to a little table on a film or TV set that is filled with snacks. To be accurate, craft services is not just the little table. It is the department responsible for keeping the little table filled with snacks.

Anyone can visit the craft service table at any time and take anything they want. And there's a lot of stuff on that table you want. Nuts, cookies, crackers, raw vegetables, dips, power bars, bananas, apples, raisins, muffins, beef jerky, gummy bears, M&Ms, coffee, tea, milk, juice, bottled water and smoothies are among the regular fare. At different times of day, they will change the selection, stocking bagels and cream cheese in the morning or cold cuts in the afternoon.

In addition to craft services, meals are served on the set. Union rules stipulate that film crews cannot be fed hamburgers or pizza. They require REAL food. So we're talking steak, chicken or fish. And because this is Hollywood, there is usually a vegetarian choice. Often there is a range of desserts.

Everything is served on real plates with silverware. A temporary dining area with tables and chairs is put out so one can enjoy a sit-down meal. Forget Paris, a film set is a movable feast.

While on location there is no chance you will miss a meal. Meal breaks are mandatory, and missing them incurs a penalty. A meal period must be no less than one half hour and no more than one hour. The first meal must be served within six hours from the time of first call. A second meal must be served no more than six hours after that. You get the idea. It's strict.

Combine this endless food parade with the copious amount of sitting around during a shoot, and you have a deadly combination. At the very least, you can gain a significant amount of weight during production, depending on your susceptibility to temptation.

Which is why the success of the mission is based on good nutrition. Business folks on the road often ignore this lesson. Hollywood embraced it, mandated it, long ago.

It works. Film sets run better when the catering rules are followed. So do your brain functions. When deprived of food, your mood and judgment are negatively affected. Hungry humans take more risks. They are also more inclined to fight.

I have witnessed this phenomenon at close range. My wife is a lovely person. I avoid her when she is hungry.

We are well served to observe the effects of the craft services table. It is a happy place. It can be best enjoyed through moderation. And it is a reminder that the mission, and life, is based on good nutrition.

McDonbel, McDouglas, McDonald's

My FIRST COMMERCIAL SHOOT for McDonald's was a disaster. The initial inkling that it might not be a great day came when the on-camera talent mispronounced "McDonald's" on the first take. He needed to recite thirty seconds of continuous copy. The screw-up came after four words.

Around take fifty-eight we had our first useable piece of film. As we moved past take seventy we realized that fifty-eight would be the only useable piece of film we would shoot.

In some ways I brought this calamity on myself. Instead of listening to Lewis Roth, the director, I sided with the agency art director and producer. Lew suggested a different actor, one he knew could handle the thirty seconds of uninterrupted copy that the script demanded.

My agency coworkers preferred the look of a different actor. And he did look good. He looked terrific standing there mispronouncing "McDonald's." Which didn't compensate for the fact that he couldn't deliver the performance we needed.

Lew knew better than we did. Of course, he did. Agency personnel might spend six or eight weeks on a set in a year. Commercial directors spend many multiples of that. That's where they live. You hire directors for the exact reason that we ignored ours.

On a shoot, my job is to protect the concept of the spot. Micromanaging the stylist or the cinematographer is a very poor use of my time. Good directors will improve your commercial. They will make it more interesting and entertaining. Listen to them. You will actually accomplish more by doing less.

That's not to say you let the shoot run on autopilot. Some directors can lose perspective as they immerse themselves into the individual scenes. I had a New York director spend an afternoon shooting a woman's lips as she bit down on a strawberry. Take after take after take, this guy shot and reshot and reshot. I had no idea what he was after. It turned out he was after the actress.

The key to a successful shoot is a well-run preproduction meeting. Typically, the pre-pro takes place a couple of days before the shoot on the day after the tech and location scouts. The day before filming is left open as a safeguard to solve any last-minute problems. All the key players get in one room: agency folks, clients, director, cameraman, stylist, wardrobe, location, props, special effects, everyone. You go over the shooting board shot-by-shot. The final shot list is set. Disagreements, problems and technical difficulties all get worked out there and then.

A great pre-pro meeting usually results in a smooth and successful shoot. I missed the pre-pro before the McDonald's shoot. Hence I stood there and watched the world collapse around me. I'm prepared for the apocalypse because of this shoot.

Commit this to memory. The key to a successful shoot is a well-run preproduction meeting.

Ultimately, a commercial was shot. A very mediocre commercial. It was a low point in my career. Every client I have worked with since owes a debt to McDonald's or McDouglas, or however you pronounce it.

The Y2K bug

BACK IN 1999, I had a speaking engagement with a division of IBM responsible for Y2K fixes. These guys were overworked and overwrought. The year 2000 was bearing down on them and Armageddon was predicted.

Do you remember the Y2K bug? Let's quickly revisit. Back in the early days of computers, programmers, to save memory, entered years by the last two digits. 1970 became 70, 1971 became 71, and so on. When the year switched to 2000, or 00, programmers thought that computers would think the year was 1900.

This tiny glitch was predicted to have catastrophic consequences. The electrical grid would fail. Communications would crash. Commerce would cease. Nuclear weapons would malfunction. Cars and airplanes would go haywire. Catholics and Protestants would marry. You get the drift. It was End of Days stuff.

As I stood in front of five hundred IBMers at the Kingsmill Conference Center in Williamsburg, Virginia, the wheel was spinning, the dice were rolling and the clock was ticking down.

My message was simple. The future will get here. Tomorrow is as certain as today. Act today as if tomorrow will arrive, and you will make tomorrow better.

The counter philosophy is to live each day as if it is your last, to live for the moment. In truth, I can argue either side of this equation equally well. But for the Y2K group, I had a better chance of collecting my speaking fee with the former. Hey, my three cats live for today. They are perfectly in the moment. And while they seem to have fun, I wouldn't want any of them to program my computer.

I faced this choice in my own life. Early in my career, I didn't like flying. Airplane trips were accomplished with numerous airborne cocktails. If the plane didn't crash, and it never did, I showed up a bit in the bag.

So I began acting as if the future–and the plane—would arrive, the theory being if the pilot got us to our destination, I would be better off if I were sober and lucid. The benefits of such an approach were greater than getting high at 35,000 feet to calm my fears.

Flying was uncomfortable without the alcoholic crutch. Turbulence seemed more dramatic. But it was a bearable experience and once we touched down, I felt better about myself.

Y2K also arrived. It barely made a ripple. Perhaps it was my speech to IBM that motivated them to stop the problem. Perhaps the problem was exaggerated. Who knows?

The future has a way of showing up. Act accordingly.

Your audience is not naked

Speaking of speaking, one of my cooler lectures was to a packed house at the Smithsonian Institution.

My first book had just been released and was climbing the bestseller lists. If you're unaware of my initial literary effort, it was titled *All I Really Need to Know I Learned from Watching Star Trek.* It's a terrific book and it's still available. You just need to look around a little to find it. Try Amazon.

After the book came out, I was invited to speak at the Smithsonian. They like Star Trek over there. An exhibit of props from the original series was one of the Air and Space Museum's most popular shows.

I'm comfortable standing in front of a group. Public speaking has always come naturally to me. I experience none of the fear that seems so common. I love it.

Funny thing about public speaking: if you can do it, it's easy. But it terrifies people who can't. There is an old Jerry Seinfeld joke that addresses this. He notes that public speaking is the No. 1 fear of Americans. No. 2 is death. Which means that if you are at a funeral, you would rather be in the coffin than give the eulogy.

As a copywriter or art director, your ability to present ideas is as important as your ability to generate them. Professional development dictates that over the course of a career you will attend numerous presentation classes. After several of these, I invented my own method.

Successful meetings or lectures demand a presenter who is in control. Preparation is key. But it all goes down the tubes if you can't stand in front of a group and communicate an idea.

When that moment arrives, here's what to do. SEE the audience. That will remind you of three simple words: Stance. Eyes. Energy.

When you SEE the audience, first establish your stance. A good public speaking stance is one where you are erect, standing tall, relaxed and ready to move. It will make you look confident and that will help you feel confident. Take your time, walk a little to the left or right and the audience will naturally follow you with their eyes.

Do not picture the audience naked. What if there is an obese guy in the first row? You want that in your head all night? Besides, you need to look the audience in the eyes. If they are naked, you'll be tempted to look lower.

The second letter in SEE is for eye contact. In a small group, you should look each audience member in the eye during the first couple of minutes of your talk. Actually, you don't have to look directly into their eyes. You can look at their eyebrows. They won't know the difference. This will set the expectation that you will look at them again. It will keep them alert and ensure their attention.

With a large group, like the hundreds in the audience at the Smithsonian, or the thousands I spoke to at the Hynes Convention Center in Boston, break the audience into smaller groups. Front left, front center, front right, back left, back center and back right. Play to each section in the first couple of minutes of the talk. Remember to revisit each group as you continue.

The third letter in SEE stands for energy. Enthusiasm also begins with *E* and is just as appropriate. For me, it's a reminder to turn my nervous energy into a positive resource. Any living being will feel a rush as they begin a presentation. Uncontrolled, it can turn into a case of nerves or drooling. Use it to project power and passion. Burning off this initial surge will help you find your voice and ease into a relaxed posture.

People will feel your energy. Your enthusiasm will convince them that you believe what you are saying—even if you don't believe it. Energy and enthusiasm are perceived as conviction.

SEE how easy that is? Get a good stance. Look everyone in the eyes during the first few moments of your presentation. Convince them you care with your energy and enthusiasm.

The evening at the Smithsonian went very well. I even took questions at the end, and the questions poured in until we ran out of time. And all of us remained fully clothed the whole time.

The English accent

AMERICANS HAVE ALWAYS BEEN charmed by an English accent. Perhaps it is genetic memory from our colonial days imbedded deep in our DNA. The British, after all, were our betters. They were the civilized society from which the rough-hewn American culture was spawned. We associate the accent with intelligence and sophistication.

This influence has continued unabated. In the previous century, Winston Churchill, the Rolling Stones and Princess Diana advanced the phenomenon.

As a child, my mother asked me what I wanted to be when I grew up. I told her I would like to be either James Bond or a member of the Beatles. My mom informed me that these were all Englishmen and we were American. A few years later, I had it figured out. I could be a member of Monty Python. Sure, they were English, but there was an American in the group!

The British are basically our big brothers. They were running the planet when we were in diapers. No matter how much time passes, that won't change. They are more worldly and cooler than we will ever be. And the fact is, we will never sound as good. How could we? It's their language.

Nowhere is this more evident than at ad agencies. We practically swoon when we hear an English accent. This accounts for the inordinate number of British receptionists. So when ya call, you know, it classes the joint up.

An English inflection is absolutely mesmerizing in a meeting. Everyone listens. Nobody interrupts. The accent is soothing and convincing. The client is captivated and buys the ads. Buys the ads!

How shallow is that? The more you think about it, the more you want to kill the guy, except he sounds so nice.

An English accent adds charisma and 50 IQ points. Want proof? Would anyone care a whit about what that stupid gecko had to say if he sounded like Jar Jar Binks? Geckos are native to New Zealand. They sound like hobbits.

There is no sense fighting it. If you have something important to sell, get a guy with an English accent to give the presentation at your meeting. Really, do it. You'll be glad you did. And if you have to, settle for an Australian.

Left brain/right brain

ASK ANY ACCOUNT GUY his No. 1 pet peeve about the creative department, and they will answer in unison: "They never work on anything until right before the deadline." Is this criticism true? Is Milla Jovovich an unlikely action star?

There are some good reasons why this is so. Writers and art directors are usually working on numerous jobs. Prioritizing according to deadline makes sense.

Another fundamental of the creative process dictates this method. You have to sort your way through a lot of bad ideas before the good ones begin to appear. Until all the stupid puns and banal approaches are traversed, inspiration hides in the shadows. There is no way to shortcut this journey. You must walk the ground. This takes time.

Besides, if you have time, use it. Time is a precious commodity. Why waste it? Even if you have a good idea, you might have a better one—a great one—right before the deadline. And if that makes the account guys uncomfortable, all the better.

There is also a theory about the brain that explains this phenomenon. I share it because I have come to believe it.

The human brain is divided into two halves, the left hemisphere and the right hemisphere. While both hemispheres are capable of doing everything, in a normal human they divide the workload.

The left side of the brain is logical and fact-oriented. Words and language reside here, as do math and science. It interprets the world in a practical fashion to keep you aware and safe. It prefers an orderly and reality-based existence.

On the right, feelings and emotion are the dominant influences. It sees the world as symbols and images, it is intuitive, impetuous and loves fantasy. The right hemisphere is less interested in details and more interested in the big picture.

So here comes a job order. The creative team reads the strategy, checks the competitive ads, talks to the account guys, and starts working.

The left brain, being the logical little dictator that it is, takes immediate control of the project. It attacks the problem methodically, looking for solutions that fit its worldview. The little dictator ignores solutions coming from the chaotic, non-logical, right side of the brain.

The left brain will happily continue down this path, creating logical but uninspired ads until it encounters some dissonance. Dissonance could come in the form of a meeting with a creative director who says, "That all you got?" Or it could come in the form of a visit from the account guys, who look and act worried. But the big kahuna that turns dissonance into panic is when the deadline is right on top of you and the creative guys realize it's now or never.

At this point, the left brain will start to freak out and turn to the right brain for help. The right brain, which will have holistically looked at the problem, will then say, "Have you thought about this?" and present the solution.

That may not be a completely accurate scientific explanation. But it is a fair description of how the process works, which has been verified by the fact that my left brain has protested the entire time I was writing this.

Anyway, the deadline is the critical element in unleashing right-brain thinking, explaining why so many of the best ideas occur only at the last second.

So, if the preceding is true, why not eliminate the middle man and institute a policy of extremely short deadlines? Hence, the right brain would jump immediately into action and the creative department would become immensely more productive.

Good question. This can work. Most ad veterans can recall a time crunch that produced great ads. The problem is that it does not work on a consistent basis. If the left brain doesn't have the time to work past the bad pun stage and the right brain doesn't have the time to puzzle with the problem, all you end up with is bad puns.

In the end, account guys are doomed to live between these twin hells. One is where the creatives produce their best work at the very last minute. The second is where quickly generated bad puns create very upset clients. Even your left brain would prefer the former.

Everybody gets fired

IF YOU'VE NEVER BEEN fired, there is no reason to feel superior. In fact, you have missed a growth-inducing experience.

Everybody gets fired. If you haven't been, it's just luck. Many nearly perfect employees find themselves in the wrong spot and get downsized. Once in a while, everybody in the joint gets sacked. It's known as going out of business. You could be the best employee on Earth, but if the company is shutting its doors, you're out.

I've been canned a couple of times. The first was as a teenager. I couldn't cut the mustard at Burger King.

Much later, I found myself in an untenable position at a small agency. I wanted to quit. My girlfriend talked me out of it. Her idea was that I had the power. "Just do anything you want," she advised. "Wait for them to fire you. You'll get severance."

This was way too inspired to argue with. I spent six happy months without a care in the world. It was a very liberating experience. I didn't have to please anyone. Come in late, leave early, drink at lunch, it was all good. When they finally got around to handing me my walking papers, there was a bonus. It was June. I hadn't enjoyed summer vacation since college, so I delayed looking for work until September. I didn't even freelance.

As a creative director, I've been on the opposite side of the table, wielding the ax rather than having my head on the block. It's not much more comfortable. There's no joy in telling folks they are no longer employed.

It is a necessary part of the job. In fact, there is a school of thought that says when you're hired as a creative director, one of your first moves should be to fire someone. Talk about getting everyone's attention.

This sounds cold-blooded, but it's not. When you take over a department, there is usually someone who needs to be fired. Everyone in the department knows who it is. Sometimes that person will raise their hand to let you know it's them. In reality, you're doing yourself, the department, and the employee a favor.

Downsizing is one of the most difficult things I have been through. I sat at a small table and fired half a dozen people, one right after the other. It was a horrible morning. These were good people who had done a good job. People I trusted. And even worse, people who trusted me. Sorry, Stephanie.

Many of them said they understood. Amazingly, some sympathized with my position. One even said, "We'll all survive." I still felt bad.

As I said, everybody gets fired. It's part of a professional career, regardless of which side of the table you sit on. Don't make too big a deal out of it. And if it's June, take at least a couple of weeks to enjoy the summer.

Everybody loses accounts

OH NO, WE LOST the account. That's a fairly benign expression. We lost the account. Doesn't sound so bad. It could turn up. Check behind the cushions on the couch in the lobby.

But losing the account means heads will roll. The effect will be dramatic and immediate. Losing the account means the agency has been fired. Sometimes it isn't the agency's fault. That doesn't make it sting any less.

Didn't we just talk about this? Everyone loses accounts. The most common reason an agency gets fired is a new marketing director is hired on the client side. The new marketing director comes in and thinks the world began the day he got the job. Nothing you did before he showed up matters.

Almost immediately he or she institutes an agency search to find a firm that will be beholden to him or her. The incumbent agency may be invited to re-compete for the account, but this is usually a formality. The account is gone.

You did great work? Yawn. You grew the business? Irrelevant. Out with the old, and in with the new. Fortunes of war.

Accounts will sometimes outgrow their agency. Does it matter that the agency was a key part of that growth? Nope. Remember the VRE? We did our job. We brought in more customers than they could handle. We paid the price.

Boredom can sometimes be a factor. After a certain length of time, the client, the agency, or both tire of the relationship. Familiarity stifles innovation. The work suffers. The agency knows all the mistakes not to make, so they never stumble across that cool piece of communication that breaks the rules. You can fight boredom. Ask anyone who has ever been married.

In fact, you can survive a new marketing director, explosive growth, even discord. And an outside factor can still cost you the account. If you have a video game account and a better game or system comes along, you're done. Bye-bye ad budget.

On rare occasions, it's the agency's fault. Understanding mistakes in advertising is easy. When the agency makes a mistake, it's the agency's fault, and when a client makes a mistake, it's the agency's fault.

Just like being fired, if you've never lost an account, chances are it's just luck. Many nearly perfect agencies lose accounts. There is no reason to feel superior. In fact, you have missed a growth inducing experience. And in this case, it better be a growth-inducing experience. Otherwise, you're out of business.

Celebrity

SPEND ANY AMOUNT OF time in advertising and you will work with celebrities. I've crossed paths with a bunch, including Kid Rock, Michael Jordan, Cal Ripken Jr., Dale Earnhardt Jr., William Shatner, The Beach Boys, 3 Doors Down and Ray Stevens. I've had Olympic gymnasts in my office and joked with Indy 500 winners.

I once saw Barbara Eden of *I Dream of Jeannie* in her underwear. In a sense, the whole country saw Barbara Eden in her underwear when she lived in that ornate bottle on Major Nelson's coffee table. My encounter was a little more personal. I accidentally walked in on a wardrobe session where Barbara was wearing only a delicate tan bra and panties. The navel hidden from the eyes of American television viewers by the network censors was clearly exposed. It was very nice. I paused and stared until a wardrobe mistress broke my trance by yelling, "Get out!"

Years later, I met Barbara at a dinner and retold the story. She was very gracious, perhaps because she didn't remember me.

What's more interesting than celebrities themselves is the reaction of folks around them. They get excited. They fawn. Sometimes they are overwhelmed by the encounter.

I've experienced this myself. During a book tour, a woman approached with a camera and asked to take my photo. It's a common request. When this occurs, I will give the camera to the next person in line and have them take the photo together with the fan that made the request, always remembering to hold up the cover of my book.

As I stood and put my arm around this woman, her knees buckled. My touch had nearly caused her to faint. As I gently caught her, I remember thinking, "Now, I can die." I had just made a woman swoon. Swoon. And I'm nobody. Believe me, I am a particularly unimpressive fellow. She didn't swoon for me. She swooned for my perceived celebrity.

It's powerful stuff, celebrity. It sells movies, television, books, magazines and lots and lots of products. The celebrity doesn't even have to be well matched to the product. I mean, Madonna's children's book flew off bookstore shelves. What were Madonna's credentials for authoring a children's book? Masturbating with a crucifix dressed as a nun? Can't wait to see the Manson children's book, Charles or Marilyn—they would both sell big.

For a long time, I resisted using celebrities in my ads. I felt that you needed a star only if you didn't have an idea. I was much too much of a creative snob to stoop to that.

However, somewhere around the time that my wife got a subscription to *Us* magazine, I began to re-examine that position. Like a spawning salmon, I was swimming upstream. There is something more important than creative snobbery: selling stuff. I made my peace with celebrity advertising.

Still, if I were going to use celebs, I would rather do it right. That means matching the personality to the product or product attribute being sold. And it means negotiating for the right dollar value.

One way to check the appropriateness of a star is a Q score. This rating measures both the recognizability and likeability of a celebrity. Combing these numbers yield a score. Tom Hanks usually ranks at the top of the list.

Other factors play a role. The market is a big factor. That's why I can say without reservation, I never saw a star in the heavens that shone brighter than Hayden Fry in Des Moines.

Who? Des Moines? Hayden Fry? Fry was the coach of the Iowa Hawkeye football team. In his home market he was a rock star, legend and superhero dressed in black-and-yellow ostrich cowboy boots and a bolo tie.

Half the town showed up to watch us shoot Hayden for a public service announcement. The crowd was eerily silent when his Texas drawl lilted across the room. When he made a half-hearted joke, the place erupted into hysterical laughter. Awestruck doesn't do it justice. I've been at events with a couple of different presidents of the United States. They did not generate as much excitement as Hayden Fry.

Of course, Fry could walk through Times Square without anyone noticing. No buzz, not a peep.

America is demonstrating an unquenchable thirst for celebrity. This new breed has no special abilities, they can't sing or dance or act or hit a baseball. Can someone tell me what talent any of the Kardashians possesses? By the way, undergoing plastic surgery is not a talent. They are famous for being famous. They cease being famous when the camera is turned off. Andy Warhol said that in the future everyone would be famous for fifteen minutes. I wish he were right. These idiots go on and on.

Understanding celebrity, how it works, how it relates to your product and how it relates to your audience is a powerful chunk of knowledge. Celebrities also come with detractors. Some of your customers will not like your choice. Expect a letter or two.

Be aware that celebrity is a double-edged sword. Events can overtake your product. Tiger Woods went from an asset to a liability in the time it takes to swing a seven iron.

My strong suggestion is to have a contract written by an intellectual property lawyer. And be absolutely sure it contains a morals or arrest clause.

So, while it's fun to be backstage, on the set, in the pits or at the after party, it cuts both ways. If you recommend a celebrity to a client, anything that celebrity does, good or bad, is your responsibility. It bears repeating: your responsibility.

Is perception reality?

"PERCEPTION IS REALITY." That piece of conventional wisdom is frequently mouthed around ad agencies. It sounds good. Might even be true, sometimes.

It's easy to understand why many ad folks believe it. Rearranging and distorting reality is our business. We manipulate words and visuals to create alternate realities where the right floor wax is the key to domestic happiness or the right shoes will make you sexier. We prey on perception. Use it for our own purposes.

When I worked on Hiram Walker liquors at Foote Cone, we introduced a vodka named Twin Sisters. In the pre-launch phase, blind taste tests were held. Consumers couldn't tell one vodka from another to any statistical significance. However, when labels were put on the bottles, all kinds of differences were perceived.

I told you earlier, what's on the bottle is more important than what's in the bottle. It works for vodka as well as perfume. Labels convinced people that one odorless, colorless and tasteless liquid was different from another odorless, colorless and tasteless liquid. The right label made the vodka "smoother."

Aha, perception is reality! Here's the rub. This is not perception; it's misperception. A conclusion of the uninformed. And it is a problem. When your best customer is a misinformed customer, you're in trouble.

In the 1980s *Rolling Stone* magazine's perception versus reality campaign made this point brilliantly. By placing an aging hippie on one side of the page under the word *perception* and a youthful professional on the other side under the word *reality*, *Rolling Stone* made the advertising world understand who their readers really were.

Rolling Stone cleverly forced the reality of their readership into the media consciousness. Reality has a way of bubbling up to the surface. It's why perfumes are among the most ephemeral brands on the market. None of them lives up to their promises. Dozens of new vodkas are introduced each year. Taste is a marketing afterthought. The name, the label, the position and the marketing campaign are the variables that determine success. Most new entrants have the shelf life of a fruit fly.

I should note that American vodkas are colorless, odorless and tasteless by law. Imported vodkas can be flavored. So there is a real difference between Stoli and Ketel One.

I should also note that there are no absolutes, vodka-related or otherwise, in advertising. Sometimes perception is your best shot. If you're in fashion advertising, I suggest quickly passing by perception and going directly to delusion.

While we're at delusion, is there anything less real on the planet than reality television? Take a group of strangers. Put them in an artificial situation. Give them a series of nonsensical tests or assignments. Have it scored by celebrities. The ratings are the only thing that is real.

Your customers may be interested in the entertainment value of the lunacy, but they know the truth. They really do. And if you're honest with them. If you can deliver what you are promising. They will reward you.

Part of the reason advertisers run away from reality is that it can be a cruel mistress. Reality can be that your sales are falling. Your product is imperfect. Your retailers or franchisees are losing faith.

Like the first step of the program says, the only way to beat the problem is to admit you have a problem. Only then can you find a solution. Don't accept perception as reality. Face reality. Understand reality. Then, deal with reality.

In an industry where we use every technique in the book to alter the perception of consumers, the absolute first rule must be: don't buy your own bullshit.

No battle plan survives contact with the enemy

WE WERE SHOOTING A piece of fruit. And I thought, to imply freshness, it would be nice if a bee were flying in the foreground. Rather than use a computer-generated bee, we decided a real bee or two would look more authentic.

The director had done this before. The solution to the shot was straightforward. Bees would be frozen. Frozen bees would be placed on a leaf in front of the fruit. Turning on the lights for the shot would warm the bees. As they warmed up, they would regain consciousness and fly away. We would capture the flying bees on film with the fruit in the background. What could be easier?

On the first take we placed a frozen bee on a leaf and waited. Sure enough, the bee warmed and began to return to life. As it slowly regained its feet, we cranked the camera to high speed. Languidly, the semi-conscious bee rose up and haltingly moved to the edge of the leaf and in slo-mo tumbled over the edge, dropping out of frame.

This process was repeated with the same results. As the insects came back to life, they bore a resemblance to the un-dead. They moved like zom-bees. None of them flew.

Our next move was less sophisticated. A grip took a couple of bees in a gloved hand and flung them into frame. This worked very well. Unfortunately, a side effect was the bees becoming quite agitated and taking their anger out on the people surrounding the camera. The crew, in turn, picked up little pieces of wood and dispatched the bees to kingdom come. The spot turned out fine.

This incident mirrors a thousand others where the best-laid plans proved useless. A friend is fond of saying, "Plans are God laughing at you." I prefer the axiom I picked up at the Pentagon. No battle plan survives contact with the enemy.

Our solution was extremely low tech, which I prefer when possible. Technology can become a master that prevents us from finding the easy way out. "We'll fix it in post" is a common phrase on sets. It refers to the practice of cleaning up mistakes in postproduction, in an edit bay or by using computer-generated graphics. The CG bays can be expensive and do not always yield the result you wish for. That's why, when possible, you should solve the problem on the set, in the real world.

It's important to have plans, to be prepared, to anticipate problems. The fact that surprises will occur does not relieve you of your obligation to begin a project as buttoned up as possible. Part of your preparation should be hoping for the best, preparing for the worst and having the ability to adapt.

A practice I employ at the beginning of any production is to set touchstones for anyone working on the spot. These touchstones take the form of adjectives. Three or four will do. They ensure that everyone on the production shares the same philosophy and has a basis for decision making.

Take the zom-bee spot. We were selling ice cream. The adjectives at the foundation of the commercial were: *fresh, sensual* and *delicious.* So, everything we did could be measured against these adjectives. If a decision met those criteria, it was probably right.

Depending on the objective of the commercial, the adjectives change. A National Guard spot might have adjectives like *professional, heroic* or *adventurous.* Sunkist Orange Soda spots were always *fun, active* and *youthful.* And on it goes.

Using adjectives makes the objective of the commercial clear to everyone on the set. Everyone from the director to the hair stylist to the guy who makes the Starbucks runs is on the same page. The strength of this approach is its simplicity. So, as the battle changes, you still win.

Subliminal advertising

THERE HAS BEEN A shelf full of books written on this subject. In my career, I have never used, been a party to, or even heard about anyone in the industry using subliminal advertising.

But that's no fun.

Subliminal advertising is a paranoid's wet dream. Finding the word *sex* in a bowl of Frosted Flakes or an ice cube is the Holy Grail for these nuts.

Here's a tip. You can find the word *sex* everywhere. You can find it in the clouds, in the pattern on your sofa, in a pile of leaves, everywhere. All it takes is a little imagination. The word *sex* is a simple pattern, a squiggly line followed by some straight lines. Try it. Right now, where you are sitting, dollars to donuts you can trace the letters *s-e-x* on something in plain sight.

Moving right along, suppose that Coca-Cola successfully hid the word *sex* in an ice cube in a Coke ad. So what? How on earth is that suppose to increase sales?

And why hide the word *sex* in a photo when you can virtually show the sex act in your ad? Abercrombie and Fitch features partially nude models in explicitly sexual situations. Subliminally writing the word *sex* in the stitching on a pair of underwear would be redundant. Besides, if you're going to have a graphic artist spend time on one of these images, why waste it sneaking a word into the stitching when you can use Photoshop to enlarge the bulge in the model's underwear?

The hysteria about subliminal advertising began in the 1950s. A scam artist named James Vicary claimed to have inserted the words *eat popcorn* and *drink Coca-Cola* onto movie screens at frame rates too fast for audiences to notice. He further claimed sales of popcorn and Coke increased significantly at the theater where these messages were shown.

After scrutiny, none of Vicary's claims proved true. No study has ever replicated his assertions. It's a myth, an urban legend, an out-and-out fabrication.

Yet, the stories persist. The concept of evil advertisers manipulating behavior by controlling the subconscious of the unsuspecting public is just too damn seductive to die.

The truth is less refined. We don't attempt to probe your subconscious, we try to beat you over the head. Advertising is a blunt instrument. Subtlety is a luxury we rarely enjoy. The idea that subliminal images or words would be more powerful than the obvious messaging of an ad is silly.

Our business is based on presenting the most compelling combination of language and imagery possible. Words are crafted. Music is composed. Film is shot. Voice-over recorded. It's an incredible amount of work, all for the single-minded purpose of getting you to buy something.

The concept that a tiny, hardly noticeable word or picture hidden in the ad would make a difference is an insult. I wish it did make an impact. We'll take any edge we can get. Unfortunately, there's nothing there. Nada. Zilch. Zip.

I am under no illusion this will stop paranoid personalities from looking for the hidden messages. They will scour the grassy knoll and Area 51 until they find *sex* written in the beards of the Elders of Zion.

No one hums the announcer

SUBLIMINAL ADVERTISING IS UNNECESSARY because a hidden persuader already exists. It hides in plain sight. It has the power to make you laugh or cry. You don't see it. You hear it. It is music.

Music reaches our brains in ways that language cannot. Babies respond to music before they comprehend words. Rhythms move your body before your consciousness notices any sound. Ever cry at a movie? Chances are the same scene without music would not produce tears.

All this makes music a powerful selling tool. It sets the mood for nearly every commercial you watch. It passes by your critical thinking and directly impacts your emotions.

Imagine a man in a room sitting at a desk writing a letter. The doorknob begins to twist, and the door slowly begins to open. Suspenseful music will convince you something terrible is about to happen. A bright uplifting melody will do the opposite. Christmas music will persuade you that Santa is about to come through that door. Suddenly, the letter is a Christmas letter.

Nothing about the scene has changed except the music. Clever manipulation of a musical score can create positive feelings about a product or negative feelings about a competitor. And it does it all without saying a word.

Music can tell an audience segment that a commercial is for them. Different genres communicate to different groups. Certain segments prefer rap, others prefer country or hard rock or oldies. Matching the musical style to the proper segment is a powerful way to gain attention from your intended audience.

Jingles have a memorability that few communication devices possess. Ever have a song stuck in your head? Imagine what it's worth to an advertiser to have their jingle lodged in there.

Collaborating with a composer to produce a musical score is one of the most enjoyable parts of the ad business. Once you settle on a style and melody line, your next choice is instrumentation. Like most of advertising, this isn't brain surgery. Instruments are selected on their ability to enhance the emotion you want to elicit.

The only thing more fun than the collaboration is the music session itself. This is instant gratification. You walk into the studio in the morning with nothing. You walk out that evening with a finished track. And if you're lucky enough to afford real musicians, you spend the day with talented professionals having a wonderful time.

I have produced hundreds of tracks in my career. It never gets old.

Musicians are not always necessary. The evolution of synthesizers has made sampling an inexpensive alternate for some sessions. A string section sample can give a score orchestral depth without the need to hire sixteen violins and twelve violas.

My preference is to use real musicians when possible. They bring ideas as well as talent to a piece. Besides, there are some things that a Kurzweil or Korg cannot do as well as real instruments.

Brass is one. Horn players use their tongues. It's almost impossible to reproduce the dexterity of a horn player's tongue. The previous sentence will, no doubt, earn me the gratitude of horn players all over the world. But it is true.

A popular alternative to creating original music is to buy an existing song and tailor it to your spot. The instant recognition of a past hit used in a new context makes a strong impression on memory. Plus, you know that the audience has a positive predisposition for the song. After all, they made it a hit. My Sunkist "Good Vibrations" commercials retracked the popular Beach Boys tune to good effect.

Commercials without music are a rarity. In my opinion, they should remain so. Music is too powerful a weapon to leave on the sideline.

No one really knows why music has such a powerful emotion impact on humans. Its mechanisms remain a mystery. One thing is certain. The effects are far from subliminal.

The Big Idea

THE BIG IDEA IS the Holy of Holies in advertising. Everyone is looking for the Big Idea. It is more sought after than WMDs were in Iraq.

So what the heck is a Big Idea? How is it different from a small or medium idea? Is vente or grande the large size?

Like all things in advertising, there is a large subjective component in any discussion of Big Ideas. A jumping-off point might be to establish your definition of "big." Putting a sign that says COLD above the soft drinks in a bodega could meet all the criteria for a Big Idea. I suppose in a bodega that FRIA might be a better sign, but let's go with COLD for now.

Anyway, if the COLD sign breaks through the clutter of the store, strongly positions the soda cooler and improves sales, that's a pretty darn big idea.

How about this? A cereal maker's sales are stagnant. Changes in the advertising campaign produce no results. The cereal maker increases the size of the spout on the box so that more cereal pours out each time a customer tilts the box. Customers run out of cereal faster. They repurchase more often. Sales go up.

You can't call that thinking outside the box. It isn't thinking inside the box either. It's thinking about the box. Regardless, I think you can call it a big idea.

Neither of the two previous examples fit the traditional definition of a big advertising idea as first proposed by David Ogilvy. Ogilvy is generally credited with creating the concept. To some degree, the phrase has grown past him, but his basic tenets still apply. A Big Idea is a strong creative approach that appeals to the customer and could last thirty years.

There are plenty of huge ideas that don't meet those criteria. "You deserve a break today" not only helped McDonald's sell billions of hamburgers, it forever changed America's concept of going out to dinner. At its core, it was just a little jingle, not a stunning or particularly strong piece of creative. It wouldn't fit Ogilvy's concept of a Big Idea any more than the COLD sign. Nonetheless, it is one of the most important advertising campaigns in history.

So how does one recognize a Big Idea? Some are obvious, like "Priceless" for MasterCard or "Got Milk?" for the California Dairy Board. Everyone with a functioning brain tends to agree that the 1960s "Think Small" campaign for Volkswagen was the very definition of a Big Idea.

My definition is no better or worse than everyone else's, but I'll take a whack. A Big Idea makes you look at a product or service in a new way.

That's pretty much it. Most Big Ideas have the following qualities: they are benefit-, not feature-oriented. Simple enough to be easily understood, minimal enough to be used in many, many different ways. Top of the list is the ability of the idea to sell lots and lots of product.

There is one other property of a Big Idea. After you live with it a while, you notice it solves more problems than it was originally created to solve. It works internally and externally, it seems to have multiple meanings, it works as well on the internet as it does on film, it makes a great phone app, it works as a business-to-business ad. Even the junior client gets it!

I don't know if I have gotten you closer to understanding what a Big Idea is. The best way to think about it is this. It's like pornography. It's hard to describe exactly, but you know it when you see it.

Big Data

I REMEMBER FEELING A little let down when I learned that Russia's famed Bolshoi Ballet means big ballet. Somehow much of the magic and sophistication evaporated. The Big Ballet, that's it? What's in a name? Well, sometimes a bit of imagination and romance.

To be fair, I later learned that Bolshoi could also translate to "big," "large," or "great." Great Ballet wouldn't have seemed so bad. But the damage had been done. It had become the Big Ballet.

Big Data is also a fairly flat sounding name. But in marketing it carries a bit of magic. The easiest way to describe Big Data is TMI, too much information.

Think about this, forty-eight hours of video are uploaded to Facebook every minute, wait that's sixty hours every minute,

I mean seventy-three hours every minute. Which means you will never be able to watch all of the cat videos.

Some estimates are that the amount of information created doubles every eighteen months. From cataloging the discovery of new planets to recording the transactions of Visa cards, the amount of information, data, that is accumulating is beyond our capacity to comprehend it.

Information is growing in volume, velocity and variety. Staying ahead of it is a virtual impossibility. So what's a mother to do?

In this simplified example, suppose you own a hotel chain and are interested in weekend stays. Your reservation system collects copious amounts of data—who booked a room, their age, their zip code and on and on and on. Plus, you can track the internet habits of anyone who visited your site.

These factors form nodes. Nodes define a particular characteristic or behavior. The nodes have edges. These edges define relationships between the nodes. Mathematicians call these "conditionally dependent" relationships. Once these conditionally dependent relationships are identified, potential weekend bookers can be identified.

Sifting though the same information, a normal marketing analysis might figure that 20 percent of previous customers might book a weekend room. But you can't predict what a specific customer will or won't do. What Big Data can tell you is what each of your previous customers is likely to do. Meaning you can focus your efforts on finding those with an 80-percent chance (or 70- to 90-percent chance) of booking a weekend room.

That is why Big Data is a big deal. Rather than working with groups or trends, it can isolate individuals.

Not to say that ad agencies have achieved this level of predictive analysis. That remains elusive, because, like the Bolshoi, the information doesn't stand still. It dances, changes over time. The best we can do is to back-test a thesis. Therefore, insight or professional judgment still plays a significant role. But we're getting closer.

In a way, Big Data connects us with our roots. Although advertising is a mass medium, messaging should always be directed to a single consumer. Written as if you're talking to a person, not a group. With Big Data, that truth is as literal as it is figurative.

The real jump will come as computing costs come down. When we can replace smart programmers with smart computers. And when agencies begin to catalogue their creative messaging in a way that can interface with sales data. That should keep us on our toes for the next few years.

Small agencies

CAN A SMALL AGENCY really be as good as a large one? Are there Jenny Craig commercials on Lifetime Movie Network? Ever hear the story of David and Goliath? Does Goliath ever win?

As I write this, I am headed to Technicolor in Manhattan. There I will tweak the final color and sound on a newly minted theater video. The director of the video is an Academy Award winner. The cinematographer has been nominated. Another Academy Award winner did the color correction. A multiple platinum recording artist wrote and recorded the music. Am I getting through to you, Mr. Beale?

The largest agency in the world cannot achieve better film production quality than my little agency in Arlington, because they can't work with better filmmakers. The top shelf is the top shelf. Bigger agencies can hire the same folks as LMO. They can do as well, but not better.

There are no better special effects companies than Industrial Light and Magic or PDI, which was owned by Dream-Works. I've worked with both of them. It's the same with photographers, composers and voice-over talent. If you have the budget, the best will line up to work for you. No one will ask the size of your agency.

If this sounds self-serving, hell, it's my book. It's also true.

What about the ads themselves? Is it possible for an advertising agency located a couple of blocks from the jail in Arlington, Virginia, to create ads that are as effective as those produced at Y&R, McCann or Saatchi? Sales speak for themselves. They don't care about the size of your agency either.

Enough with the questions. An ad agency is the minds of the people who work there. There are talented writers and art directors everywhere in this country. Some of the best do not like the big agency environment or being a cog in a huge machine. Not everyone loves New York. I do, but different strokes.

Naturally, there are many differences between big and small agencies and advantages and disadvantages to both. Large agencies like to tout their media clout. But that media clout is most useful to clients that could not be serviced at a small agency. Budweiser, for example could not be handled by a small agency. Which doesn't matter, because if a small agency won Budweiser, it would cease to be a small agency. Once they started buying media for Budweiser, that formerly small agency would have as much media clout as anyone in the country.

Size matters, but chemistry matters a lot more. Finding an agency that shares your philosophy and is highly motivated will yield a stronger, more profitable relationship.

If you decide to award your account to a large international corporate conglomerate, that entire company will not work on your business. That huge agency will set up a small agency inside their megabusiness. The actual number of folks assigned to your account will be much smaller than the total number at the mega-agency, and the number of folks who work day-to-day on your business will be fewer than that. It will in almost every way resemble a small shop, the exception being that they will assign six account guys to do the work of two.

It's actually easier for a small agency to accommodate a large account than for a large agency to accommodate a small one. At a large shop, small accounts are small fry. Common sense and good financial practice demand that the very best people work on the most profitable accounts. A ten-million-dollar account at a billion-dollar agency will find its own level, which will not be the penthouse.

A small shop can usually scale up to handle a bigger client. A twenty-million-dollar account that joins a thirty-million-dollar agency immediately becomes the big dog. Everyone at the agency, including top management, is at full attention. The level of service will reflect that.

Not everyone is comfortable at a small agency. Some client egos will never fit through the door of a smaller shop. That's fine. It is important to know who you are.

But a tape measure is a poor way to evaluate an ad agency. An agency should be chosen with your head and your heart and by their head and heart. And remember Goliath was larger, but David had a bigger heart.

The lowest form of advertising

HERE IS A VALUABLE piece of information. It will allow you to evaluate the level of service you are receiving from your ad agency.

If at any time during a creative meeting any of the following three ideas appear, your account is getting short-sheeted.

Bad idea #1 is the soap opera commercial. It is supposed to be funny. Dramatic over-acting will be accompanied by cliché organ music and sexual innuendo. This lame idea has been trotted out a million times before, never works and is painful to watch.

Bad idea #2 is the game show. This is another terrible attempt at humor. The host will be obnoxious. The winner will be orgasmic. The results will be unimpressive.

Bad idea #3 is the mime commercial. This is supposed to be clever. Mimes don't talk. They don't sell either. By the way, don't be fooled by the Blue Man Group. They are mimes that are painted blue instead of white.

Although these ideas are numbered one through three, they all suck equally. They're not even advertising, they're badvertising. It is absolute proof positive that the people working on your account are the most junior folks in the shop.

If your agency trots out any of these insipid, uninspired concepts, take it as a direct insult. They are screaming in your face, "We don't give a fig about your account."

There is only one reasonable reaction. Start an agency review immediately.

Werner Heisenberg

No, HE WASN'T THE dean of Faber College. He was a Nobel Prize–winning physicist best known for his theory called the uncertainty principle.

Basically—which means I'm about to butcher this—the uncertainty principle states that the more precisely you measure the position of a particle, the less precise the measurement of the momentum of said particle becomes, and vice versa. In English, the act of measuring something changes the something you are measuring. This theory, which was invented to describe actions on a subatomic level, is one of the bedrocks of quantum mechanics.

Uncertainty is less precisely defined in advertising but every bit as certain. An old advertising saw says, "I know half of my advertising budget is wasted, I just don't know which half. That quote, often attributed to Robert Townsend, the legendary chairman of Avis, is as true as Heisenberg's formula.

We know advertising works. We can tell that by results. We just can't tell exactly how those results came into being.

A guy wakes up in the morning and gets ready for work. Watching the morning news, he sees a television commercial for Joe's Plumbing. Driving to work, he hears the Joe's Plumbing jingle on the radio. At work, a Joe's Plumbing internet banner pops up on his computer. On the way home, he becomes stuck in traffic behind a Joe's Plumbing truck. Passing the truck, he also passes a Joe's Plumbing billboard.

Upon arriving home, he discovers the toilet is backed up. He uses Google on his smartphone and finds the number of a plumber. It's Joe's. He calls and makes an appointment. Before he hangs up, the dispatcher asks him where he found out about Joe's Plumbing. The guy answers without hesitation, Google.

So which of the advertising efforts of Joe's Plumbing was responsible for the call? The commercial, the radio jingle, the billboard, the paint job on the truck, the spider in the search engine? Which was it?

I say it was all of them. Because if you remove one, the guy might have called Larry's Plumbing. Then again, the message might have been more important than the media. That clever Joe's Plumbing jingle might have done the trick. Or not. Or maybe it was both. Or neither.

When one looks at all the variables, there is more certainty in Heisenberg's principle of uncertainty than there is in advertising. Two plus two always equals four in his universe. Depending, of course, on the act of measuring it.

Advertising is still trying to figure out if it is on the art side of business or on the business side of art. No one should confuse it with a science. That much is certain.

Every job is a job

I WAS SITTING IN the office of the director of a mental health facility in Tinley Park, Illinois, when the telephone rang. The director waved his hand to let me know he was going to take the call. For the next few minutes he squirmed uncomfortably and rarely spoke. When he did, it was in conciliatory tones. I'll never know if the conversation came to an amiable resolution. I do know the exchange was handled in a calm and professional manner.

After he hung up the phone, we didn't return to our previous topic. Instead, he rotated his chair toward me and held up two fingers. "That's number two," he said.

"Every day," he paused, "when I walk into this office, I know I'm going to receive three bad phone calls. That was number two today. I can expect one more. If it doesn't come, it's a good day. Tomorrow, I might get four."

I didn't respond but was attentive, and he continued.

"This is a tough job. Every decision I make gets second-guessed, and it is impossible to please everyone. A lot of these people have legitimate complaints. It used to eat me up. I finally realized I couldn't function if I let these calls bother me."

I thought this attitude reflected very well on his mental health. Every job has good and bad parts. A ditch digger gets to work outside. His physical labor keeps him in shape and he can count on a tan. Of course, rainy days are less than pleasant.

Prepare for the rough patches; they are part of the job. They are part of every job.

If you love to write, copywriting is a great job. But it can be very frustrating. For every idea that flies, a thousand are in the trash can. And you can't even use the trash can. All white paper must go into the recycling bin. All this rejection can sour you on something you love.

Which brings us to a common piece of conventional wisdom. Find a job you love, and you'll never work a day in your life. Not true. Even the job you love will have tedious, difficult and outright horrifying days.

And then there is this: if you find a job doing the thing you love, you may turn the thing you love into a job. That, my friends, is the opposite side of the coin.

Speaking of flipping things around, even a bad job will have great parts. Sometimes that's only payday. However, payday is rarely an insignificant factor when choosing employment.

You can prove this with a simple test. Stop paying your employees, and see how long they keep showing up.

Another way to go is to find the job where you can make the most money. Then you can use the freedom that money buys to do the things you love. There is no right choice. There is only the right choice for you.

Personally, I can't imagine doing any other job than writing, whether it's behind the desk at an advertising agency or banging away at my home computer with a cat under my chair. Still, I know there will be times when love is not the right word to describe my feelings toward my profession. On those occasions, I think about payday.

All business is personal

GET USED TO THAT idea. Embrace that idea. Understand and employ it. All business is personal because all business takes place between persons. The human element is the only element that conducts business. It is impossible to separate humans from commerce.

In fact, if someone ever says to you, "It's not personal. It's just business," prepare to get screwed in the most personal way possible.

Think about the best business relationships of your career. People you liked and respected surrounded you. Moreover, you were working with people you trusted. Those are qualities found in humans, not on spreadsheets.

I once worked on the largest bank in the mid-Atlantic region. The founder and CEO, B. F. Saul, was a very impressive and accomplished individual who was on the *Forbes* list of the richest Americans.

Our meetings took place in the bank's conference room around a beautiful boardroom table that was six feet wide and forty feet long. Mr. Saul, Mr. Boyle, the bank's vice-chair, and I were the only ones seated at the table. The thing I remember most about those gatherings in that very large, mostly empty room was that the meetings felt intimate.

One instance stands out. As we were leaving the room at the end of a presentation, Mr. Saul reached over my shoulder and turned down my suit collar, which had popped up during the meeting. He smiled and said, "There you go." There was something very sweet about it. It was a moment of genuine warmth. Just something you would do for a friend. Make no mistake, we were not close and we certainly weren't equals. I always called him Mr. Saul. He called me Dave. But our discussions were honest and respectful, and I never doubted he wanted me to succeed. We worked our butts off on Mr. Saul's bank because he made us believe he cared about us.

A relationship with a client has to be nurtured. You are either growing closer or further apart. If it is not becoming more harmonious, it is becoming more dissonant. I know the direction I want the relationship to take with my clients.

I'll go a step further. An ad agency should love its clients. L-O-V-E, *love* its clients. They are the very reason for our existence. Without them we are nothing. We have no purpose, no income, no anything.

Incomprehensively, I have worked at agencies that openly expressed their hatred for certain accounts. I won't name any names. Gallo.

It is impossible to produce great work on an account you hate. Why stay late at night? Why deploy more resources? Why go the extra mile? Professionalism demands you do a good job. Professionalism doesn't demand you miss dinner with your wife to work on a client you hate.

I guarantee that the worst experiences of your professional life all have one thing in common. Some idiot you couldn't stand.

At LMO, I demand that our employees find something they like about every client. You might have to dig to discover it, but there is something to like about everyone. I promise you, it's there.

Not only is this critical in motivating employees, but clients know when they are not liked. It's impossible to hate a client and pretend you like him or her. William Shakespeare said that thoughts have wings. Your thoughts will be revealed. If you dislike a client, something will give you away, and that something may cost you the account.

Find a trait, a feature or a quality that you like. And it better be real. Once you do that, you can start giving your clients the service they deserve.

All business is personal, whether you are picking up dry cleaning, signing expense checks or giving the most important new business presentation of your life. It will always come back to people.

Your true agenda

I ONCE SPENT A summer skydiving. Friends asked why I would jump out of a perfectly good airplane. Trust me, the planes I jumped out of were far from perfectly good.

These were not tandem jumps. I was not attached to the belly of an expert to keep me safe. They opened the door, I leapt out alone and was alone in the air.

I was a rotten skydiver. My body position stunk. I constantly missed the landing zone. Ten jumps went by before they let me off the static line. That's the training device used before you are allowed to pull your own cord. One end of the line is attached to the plane and the other end is attached to your ripcord so that it automatically pulls the chute as you exit the plane. In skydiving vernacular, the static line is called "the dope rope." The average number of jumps on the dope rope before they let you pull your own cord is three. Like I said, I took ten.

Tim, my jumpmaster, told me a bag of dog food could hold a better aerodynamic position than me. Well, he didn't actually say dog "food."

Thinking back, part of the problem was that I never told Tim the real reason I took up skydiving. Fear of heights had plagued me since I was a kid. If I had mentioned this phobia to Tim, perhaps he would have adjusted my training in some way. I never told him. I figured I could just tough it out. After all, my goal was to overcome my fear of heights. What better way than jumping out of an airplane, pretending to be brave? Stupid, huh?

Early in the book, I talked about Jovan. I promise this is my last Jovan story. They produced beautiful, expensive commercials but hardly bought any media time.

For the copywriters, like myself, this was a blessing and a curse. We got to write clever, award-winning television commercials. Fly to the coast to produce them. Then no one would ever see them.

The real targets of the spots were department store buyers. Dick Meyer (you recall Dick) would stage incredible sales shows. Buyers from around the country would attend. Our commercials would be shown on twenty-foot screens flanking the stage.

So when we created commercials for Dick, we knew that they had to look good projected onto huge screens. Subtle was not in our dictionary. Giant images on these huge screens augmented by a deafening sound system would whip the buyers into frenzy and they bought huge amounts of Jovan products for their stores.

Dick was very upfront that this was his objective. He let everyone working on the account know that the sales show was the real endgame. Because we knew his true agenda, we created spots appropriate to the venue. The result was a success.

There is a lesson here for every brand manager on earth. If you want your advertising to achieve its objective, you must share your true agenda with your agency—your true agenda. Jovan told us how the commercials would be used, and we created spots that fit the bill.

ServiceMaster is a franchise-based company that cleans rugs and repairs flood and fire damage. An important part of their business is to sell franchises. So when we created television commercials for ServiceMaster, the agenda was broader than displaying our services and attracting customers. Part of the job was to attract new franchisees.

With that in mind, we portrayed ServiceMaster technicians, managers and supervisors in the most heroic light possible. The result was that the spots not only produced increased sales for ServiceMaster, but franchise sales also jumped. This was possible only because ServiceMaster shared their full objective, selling franchises, with the agency.

I could cite more examples. It all comes to the same thing. Share your true agenda with your agency, and they will be able to train their full resources on the problem.

The opposite is also true. Hide your true agenda from your agency, and it becomes impossible for them to solve the problem.

One of the most idiotic phrases in business is: "You don't need to know." Keeping people in the dark, withholding information or leaving out important details because your agency doesn't need to know is worse that counterproductive. It is self-sabotage.

If I had to go through my skydiving experience again, my opening line to Tim would have been, "I'm here because I have a fear of heights and hope that facing this fear is a way to overcome it." Would it have made a difference? Did I sabotage myself? We'll never know. But I can't help but think I would have been a better skydiver if I made my jumpmaster a better teacher by telling him my true agenda.

One last thing

THIS BOOK IS NEARLY done, but advertising is never finished. It is a journey, not a destination. While agency clients tend to fall into two camps, goods or services, advertising is neither. It is a process, a constantly evolving process.

Advertising is comparable to lawn care. You mow the grass, edge the lawn, kill the weeds, and your front yard looks marvelous. To maintain this attractive appearance, you need to do it again next week and the week after that.

Miss a week, and the grass gets long, the edges get ragged, weeds pop up all over. The beautiful impression you have created is gone. No one remembers the immaculate yard you once slaved over. They see only the unkempt plot in front of your home.

Advertising is the front lawn of a company. It is the face that a business puts forward for the public to see. Like a lawn, it must be constantly maintained. It will have to survive severe weather and droughts. The seasons will change. There will be times of growth and decline. Through it all, the chore never ends.

The chore is dirty, sweaty and varied. Advertising is an untidy process. You need to be at ease with the chaos, the false steps, the difficult circumstances. They are an important and unavoidable part of the process.

Even when the process is being smoothly managed, internal politics or market forces can intervene. Change is constant. Anticipation gives way to reaction. It's a mess.

There, I've said it. The process of advertising is a mess. That's how you know you're doing it right. Your hands are dirty.

You have to explore dead ends. To find a course of action by getting off track. To take advantage of the opportunity that didn't exist when the strategy was written. To be open to ideas no matter who proposes them, the junior copywriter or even the receptionist.

None of this mess should be visible to your customers. Your creative product should look consistent and polished. Like a duck on a pond, you should look like you are moving effortlessly, but under the water, you should be paddling like hell, kicking up algae and mud and making a mess of things.

When I decided to write this book, I decided to show advertising with all its warts. People create advertising, and people are imperfect. As I've shown, agencies and clients can be motivated by things that have nothing to do with advertising or customers. Sometimes we don't understand our own motivations.

I've found one common element in great ad people. They take the work seriously, but they don't take themselves seriously. This is not a business for perfectionists. It is a hands-on, get-it-done, make-it-work, do-the-best-we-can-in-the-time-we-have-and-then-move-on business. There is never a finished product.

Every advertising problem has an infinite number of creative solutions. There is no best answer. At some point, you need to make a decision based on professional judgment, a subjective decision.

Research-based decisions are no different. They are the subjective opinions of your customers. They provide clues, not answers. Your professional judgment is still required.

The good news, as we have discussed numerous times in this book, is that even bad advertising works. While I'm not suggesting you purposely create bad ads for your product, bad ads are better than no ads.

Good ads work even better. Pay attention to the fundamentals. Segment your audience. Sell benefits, not features. Appeal to both the head and the heart. Tell your audience what it wants to hear.

A few years back, I read a survey of America's favorite commercials. The list contained spots by McDonald's, Budweiser, AT&T and IBM. All the "favorites" were for some of the top advertising spenders in the industry. I realized the list didn't reflect the quality of the commercials; it measured the quantity of advertising. The companies that mowed their lawn every day were perceived as having the best ads.

These companies treat advertising as an ongoing process. Their advertising is constantly changing and being refreshed. Yes, their creative is good, but it is not the crucial factor in their brand image. For, if any of them stopped mowing the lawn tomorrow, it wouldn't take long for the weeds to take over and undo everything they have accomplished.

There you have it, my thirty-plus years in a relatively neat bundle. I consider myself lucky. I've sold a ton of stuff. Experienced highs and lows. Won accounts worth tens of millions of dollars. Lost 'em too. Had wonderful and awful clients. Watched the sun rise after sleepless nights. Helped build an agency. Laughed, cried and nearly died with hundreds of co-workers, many of whom have become friends.

And if you're ever interested in mowing the lawn, I have a mower.

Acknowledgments

Bob Jones, Bob Ebel, Bill Pittman, Norm Porter, Millie Olsen, Tom Tawa, David Blueman Innis, Ray Helmers, Larry Butts, John Trusk, Ralph Rydholm, Steve Nubie, Jenny, John McKee and our Miss Laura Kaiser. The Marks Brothers, Modesto and Puccini, Harvey, Mitch Ingel, Bruce Bendinger, Joe Guerra, John Babyman Espinoza, Dean Bastian, Kathy Grisham and Scott Shellstrom. Bob Kane and Ray Lewis in ATL, Cleveland Raine Willcoxon III, B. A. Albert, Joey Reiman, Ward Wixon, Andi Arnovich, Jim Greenwood, Denzil Stickland, Caroline McConnell Strickland, Shaun Allen, Johnnie Jack Noone, Joe Landy, Mike Bollinger, Nancy Willis, Allison Mobley, Jim Kinglsey and Dean again. The Gorn. Señor Rober Connelly. Everyone at LMO past, present and future. Jane Cavolina. My editor, Cal Barksdale.

To and for everyone named Marinaccio or Grillo and some named other things like Brennen, Granfield or Wilson Howarth.

And my deepest gratitude to anyone who has ever been a client.

Index